THROWN AWAY CHILDREN

Eden's Story

Louise Allen

with Theresa McEvoy

MIRROR BOOKS

First published by Mirror Books in 2020

Mirror Books is part of Reach plc
10 Lower Thames Street
London EC3R 6EN

www.mirrorbooks.co.uk

Print ISBN 978-1-913406-48-6
eBook ISBN 978-1-913406-50-9

Typeset by Danny Lyle

Printed and bound in Great Britain by
CPI Group (UK) Ltd, Croydon, CR0 4YY

A CIP catalogue record for this book is available from the British Library.

Every effort has been made to fulfil requirements with regard to
reproducing copyright material. The author and publisher will be
glad to rectify any omissions at the earliest opportunity.

1 3 5 7 9 10 8 6 4 2

Cover image: Shutterstock
(Posed by model)

THROWN AWAY CHILDREN

Eden's Story

No Excuses.

There are no excuses for
child abuse and neglect.

There are no excuses for why a
child is experiencing trauma.

Trauma shows itself both loudly and quietly,
sometimes you would never know it was there.

And no adult who has experienced that
trauma should feel that it is okay to pass on.

A bad childhood is not an excuse

To those who have influence, power and profession
– you have no excuse allowing it to continue.

To the ones who choose to abuse and
neglect children – you have no excuse.

There are no excuses for the
way we treat some children.

I write my books for those children, whether
still young or grown, who know things that
others don't and hopefully never will.

Contents

The cases I reveal in my books are all based on true experiences, but I have changed names and some details to protect their identities as they go on to build new lives and families of their own.

Part One

Ashley

I

Ashley swings on the back two legs of the kitchen chair, bare feet brushing the floor, and scrolls idly through memes and images on her phone's feed, 'liking' the odd post here and there.

She sees that she is invited to 'follow' a new floristry business that has just been opened by a friend of a friend. Fair enough. It seems brave going into business by yourself; good on her. And working with flowers sounds like a lovely thing to do. It has been a long time since anyone bought Ashley flowers. A nightclub has opened up on the Brampton Road where the old Octopussy wine bar used to be. A bunch of her old crowd are heading there tonight to check it out. Priscilla has updated her status to 'in a relationship'. Alright for some.

Looking great hun, she comments beneath the story of an old school friend who she hasn't seen anything of for a couple of years, who has posted an image of her freshly and perfectly manicured acrylics in close-up. They do look really good, actually. Ashley clenches her own fists shut in order to avoid witnessing the chewed nails and split cuticles that make for a poor comparison.

She glances absently down from her seventh-floor window to the little ant people below, scurrying around down there, getting on with their business. She wonders how people are able to have so much urgency in them. They all look so very busy, all on their way somewhere. She feels none of that. Nothing but lethargy. Sometimes seven floors feels just too high up to bother even to leave the flat and take Eden to the park for some fresh air. It is easier to stay put. Everything seems like hard work. Besides, she has nothing to rush for.

Right now Eden is fast asleep, enjoying her mid-morning nap in the next room. Ashley has about another 20 minutes or so of this guilt-free part of the day when she can engross herself in an online world until Eden wakes up. And actually she knows it won't be long before Eden grows out of even having this short sleep in the day, and Ashley will have no time at all to herself. Normally she does make an effort to put the phone away for as much time as she can when Eden is up and about. She has read somewhere that she shouldn't really be looking at a screen at all in front of Eden; her daughter should have her undivided attention. But then, on the other hand, what does an 18-month-old toddler know or care, really?

More scrolling and swiping. Another friend, Dana, has made a batch of cupcakes, all beautifully frosted with elaborate flower-shaped decorations. They look amazing, almost too good to eat. Perhaps Ashley should try some baking for a change. She used to enjoy it. Baking with Nana years ago, making pastry for jam tarts and pies, mixing eggs and fat and flour for Victoria sponges and fairy cakes. Why not do some of that again? It would do her – and Eden – some good. She can't remember the last time she baked anything. Kitchen adventures these days mainly revolve around batch cooking – purees initially, from when Eden was about six months old; now bolognese or macaroni cheese that she can put into smaller portions and freeze. Cooking that is practical and necessary, but not fun or creative. She hasn't baked anything like that since Nana died, before Eden was born.

It's been a long time since she's seen Dana too, Ashley thinks. She has kind of lost touch with most of the old faces. Having a baby isolates you.

The phone pings an alert, distracting her from that train of thought. It is from Christina, with her daily psychic update and advice.

Don't be too critical of yourself, Ashley. I know from our psychic reading last month that you have an awful lot of unused potential which you have not taken advantage of yet. Try something new today. A flower will become significant. Sometimes your introverted nature means that people see you as wary and reserved. Try to relax so that you are more sociable.

Chance would be a fine bloody thing, Ashley thinks. There's no one to be sociable *with*. But Christina is right. She always hits the nail on the head. It's amazing how much these psychics can tell about you from just a few details about your life. Ashley does have a tendency to be too wary – of people, of going out, of trying new things. Perhaps she should live a little. It's the 21st century. Having a baby doesn't have to mean the end of your social life. She should make the effort to get out more. Relax, like Christina says. It isn't healthy to be cooped up here all the time with a kid in such a tiny space. She is on the waiting list to move; a one-bedroom flat won't be ideal once Eden is toddling around, but it's been fine for just the two of them, for now. In some ways, it makes it easier to keep an eye on Eden. She's always in view, always close by, always safe. It's just that being stuck all the way up here doesn't really help very much with meeting people and being part of a community. Ashley remembers, with a rueful smile, how she used to think it would be so much fun to live in a tower block. All those people so close together – how sociable it would be. The reality is somewhat different. Ashley has never felt as lonely as during this last year, with no Nana to help her through. But her own mother managed to bring up a child on her own, and Ashley is determined to do the same. *But Mum had Nana to help her*, the little voice inside her head reminds her, *while you have no one*.

She moves to the sink and rinses out her coffee cup, leaving it to drain on the side. In a fit of determination, she adds flour and eggs to the wipe-clean shopping list attached to the front of the fridge. Fairy cakes are straightforward. Quick and easy. It's been an age since she last made them, and most importantly, Eden will like them and like helping to make them. Next, she forces herself to sort through the laundry basket and put another load of washing on: mostly Eden's clothes and sleep suits, and cot-sheets. Ashley finds that she hardly seems to have any clothes any more. Nothing new, anyway. She feeds the cactus plant that is looking a little sorry for itself on the window ledge, and checks her phone again. 'Thanks hun, catch up soon,' the school friend with the nice nails has replied. *Put the bloody phone down*, Ashley tells herself. Nobody's interested in you. She hears the thud of the mail falling through the letterbox onto the mat and heads into the tiny hallway to retrieve it. Something from the council. A postcard from Tessa in Lanzarote. That's nice. She didn't think anyone sent postcards any more. An offer on pizza delivery — she doesn't know why they put them through the door anyway, no company will come up this far in the flats to actually deliver to the door. A copy of the local free newspaper, from which a load of junk mail immediately spills. A flyer for that new night club, the White Orchid — announcing free entry for one night only and a promotional deal on drinks.

There is a flash of yellow across the front of the newspaper, announcing in-depth horoscopes on page 18. *Find out what today holds in store — and how your life is going to change over the next few weeks.* Ashley sighs. Eden won't wake for a few more minutes. Time enough to take a look — it can't hurt. Her mother always disapproved of her fascination with the zodiac, but then her mother died a long time ago, long before

Nana, and isn't around to know. Ashley thumbs through the pages until she reaches page 18. She scans the entries and finds 'Aries' quickly.

Change is on the horizon for you. The world is about to turn upside down. But the responsibility is yours, which means that it is up to you to make it happen. Right now, your destiny is in your hands. You will soon meet someone special, but it will take you out of your comfort zone to get there. The effort is worthwhile. Go for it!

She has to get out of here, even for a short time. So why not? It is up to her to make it happen. How true. Nothing is going to happen while she is stuck here seven floors up with a toddler. There is zero chance of meeting anyone unless she goes out. Ashley reaches for her phone and sends a tentative message to Kerry, the one remaining good friend who she is in regular contact with. The only one who didn't desert her shortly after Eden was born – who has helped her out in the past and might just babysit if she isn't busy tonight.

The reply comes back within a minute.

'4 U, Ash? Course! Going somewhere special?'

Ashley reaches for the nightclub flyer and takes a quick snapshot to send back in reply. Her mind is made up. It will take a bit of courage to invite herself along with the group who are heading there, but 'change is on the horizon', and that needs to begin from within. Now, what to wear? And what to do with her hair?

That's Eden stirring now. All too soon it is time to be back on duty as a mum. But, were anyone there to see it, there is a new spring in Ashley's step: a little more energy as she heads towards the bedroom, a little hope. Today *will* be the start of something new, something big. She can feel it.

'Come here, darling! Give Mummy a cuddle. That's it. Did Eden have a nice nap? Let's get you out of there, shall we?'

The usually long afternoon goes by in a flash for once, with something to look forward to and something to do. Ashley manages to paint her nails, wash and blow dry her hair, and dig out a pair of stretchy black jeans that look surprisingly good – she has regained most of her pre-baby figure – paired with black ankle boots that she has forgotten she had. A couple of episodes of *Peppa Pig* – why are they so short? – help keep Eden occupied while Ashley gives herself a mini-makeover. Eden seems to like them on repeat, and doesn't mind if she already knows what happens; in fact, she seems to prefer it. Ashley can hear her babbling away at the television as though in conversation with the characters on screen.

Ashley tags herself into the group going to the nightclub, and is pleased with the comments from old friends that sound genuinely welcoming and happy that she is coming along.

'Wow! You look brilliant, Ashley!' Kerry says, out of breath, when she arrives early in the evening for her baby-sitting duties.

'Thank you!' Ashley is really pleased at the compliment. She has enjoyed getting ready for this rare treat of a night out. She notices Kerry's panting. 'Are you ok? Did you walk all the way up the stairs?' Her heart sinks, just a little bit. 'Is the lift not working again? I haven't been out yet today.'

'No, it's fine – I just thought it would be a good way to get my steps up today – but the novelty wore off after the third floor and I'm rather regretting that decision, to be honest!'

They giggle together.

'I almost wish I was going with you, though. You really do look stunning! I haven't seen you all dolled up in a while.'

'I thought it was about time I made the effort. I wish you were coming, too. But you know you're the only one I could really trust with Eden.' She gives Kerry a little squeeze. 'We'll have a good night in together soon, though, instead. A proper catch up. How's that? And a drink together now. It will give me a bit of Dutch courage. I need a little bit of confidence to start the night.'

'Confidence, my foot. They'll be falling at your feet. Look at you!'

Ashley asks about school. Kerry is a Year Two teacher in one of the local primaries, still in her first year of teaching, and always has a silly story to relate about what the kids have been up to.

As they share a bottle of wine, Ashley explains Eden's routine carefully. It's been a good while since Kerry last babysat, and things change fast from baby to toddler. 'Anyway, she's ever so good with sleep these days. She's been going right through for a couple of months now. You shouldn't hear a peep out of her.'

'Bless her. You're so lucky with her, honestly. She's so good – such a poppet!'

'I know.' Ashley checks the time on her phone. She needs to get going if she's going to be in time to meet the others before they go into the club. 'She's been down since about half past six, so she'll be well asleep by now, and she almost always sleeps through.' Ashley beckons Kerry towards the bedroom, where Eden's cot is tucked away in the corner. The light in the hallway illuminates the room enough so that they can both see, just as Ashley predicted, that Eden is fast asleep, thumb dropped away from her mouth a little where she must have been soothing herself as she dropped off.

'A little drink of milk will calm her and send her back off to sleep if she does happen to wake up,' Ashley whispers. 'Which she won't! I promise. But you can call me if that happens. I'll keep checking my phone.'

'Listen, you. Just go out and enjoy yourself. Don't worry about me and Eden back here. We'll be absolutely fine. Tonight's about you. I'm really glad you're doing it. I haven't seen you like this, all ready for a night out, in ages. And really good on you for doing this by yourself. I admire your guts. So – just go! Get out of here!' Kerry is physically propelling her away from the bedroom and towards the front door of the flat.

'I'll be back by one at the latest. I promise. Probably won't last that long, actually. I'm such a lightweight, and it's been that long since I last went clubbing!'

'Don't worry about the time, honestly. Things will only just be getting going by then. I'll curl up here on the sofa, catch up on the soaps and then fall asleep. You get yourself on to that dance floor, girl.'

Ashley feels a little wobbly as she reaches for the door latch. 'I think that wine has already gone to my head!' She gives her friend an impetuous kiss on the forehead. 'Thanks, Kel. I'll make the most of it. I owe you.'

In fact, it's gone two o'clock in the morning by the time Ashley tumbles back through the doorway and noisily rouses Kerry from her slumber on the couch.

'Kerry, Kerry. Wake up. You're not going to believe what's happened. I've had the best night ever.'

'What?' Kerry's voice is drowsy and it takes her a moment to shake herself awake and respond.

'Don't be cross, with me, Kel. I'm so sorry I'm late, but I couldn't help it. I got chatting with someone. Someone nice. One of the partners involved in setting up the club. Like, one of the actual owners. I really like him!'

'That's brilliant, Ash. I'm really pleased that you've met someone. You deserve some good luck. And I'm glad it was a good night. So, the club's worth a look, is it?'

'Yeah, they've done a good job. It's got a real industrial vibe.'

In fact, the White Orchid is a sprawling temple of urban chic. The building has been stripped right back to its warehouse roots, leaving no trace of the previous, rather tacky nightclub that it has replaced. It is as if the entire inner workings of the building are on display. Exposed brickwork from floor to ceiling, uncovered air-conditioning ducts and a maze of copper pipes give it a retro, grungy atmosphere, totally in contrast to the delicate white orchids that adorn each table and curl round every architectural feature. The young crowd wear a uniform of Abercrombie & Fitch and drink champagne cocktails from olive jars.

'I'll have to get down there myself and take a look.'

'You'd love it; it's attracted a really different crowd from before. Very cool. It's all Baz's design.'

'Go on then, show us a picture of the gorgeous one.'

'Oh, no, I didn't take one,' Ashley says. 'He's very camera shy. But he's beautiful. Just perfect. He works out all the time. And he's, well I suppose he's quite the hipster.'

'I get the picture. Beard, or handlebar moustache, then?'

Ashley giggles. 'Beard.'

'Wow. Look at the time! I don't suppose you asked the cab to wait?'

'Yes, don't worry. He's downstairs waiting, holding on for you. And, lucky us, it's all paid for. Baz — that's the club-owner's name — insisted on taking care of it himself. It's all on account with the club. I'd suggest going down in the lift this time, though. Oh, Kerry, he's gorgeous. I know it's only one night, but I might be in love. It's written in the stars, I know it is. I think he could be the one!'

It is only once Kerry has gone and she has waved the taxi away (pointlessly from seven floors up, because who could see the wave – but she *has* had a bit to drink, along with what Baz described as a 'little livener' at the club, and the thought that she is waving pointlessly makes her giggle again for some reason) that she realises that she forgot to ask anything about Eden. She hadn't even mentioned her daughter after having been away from her for the whole evening! Ashley dashes to the bedroom with a sudden pang of anxiety, but of course, Eden is sleeping peacefully, thumb still near to her face in an almost identical position to before.

In the morning, Ashley has a hangover. A cracking one. It has been a long time since she has felt this rough, but at the same time there is an unmistakable familiarity to the sensation. It presents itself firstly as a blinding pain over her right eye, along with a sticky mouth so parched of saliva it makes the Sahara Dessert seem lush and fertile. Ashley lifts her head off the pillow but almost immediately falls back down into the linen with a groan. She is also starving hungry, she realises – but at the same time feels that there is absolutely no way she could put food into herself. She remembers now the way cocaine does that to you – even just a line or two.

But it is so, so worth it, no question. She has a little fizz in her stomach when she thinks about Baz. She clenches her sheet as a little squirt of excitement shoots through her. They just seemed to hit it off completely. The proffered 'livener' in his private office meant that she was far more garrulous than usual. And it gave her an inflated feeling of confidence. She remembers feeling like she could take on the whole world last night. Did she go back for a second? Possibly. In between the champagne and cocktails it is all a bit of a blur. And the wine. She mustn't forget all the wine. She'd already had a skinful before she left the house: the best part of half a bottle with Kerry.

But Baz, Baz, Baz – he's gorgeous. The name buzzes round her mouth. Bazzzzz.

She looks over to the corner of the small room. Eden is smiling up at her from between the bars of her cot, full of joy and a toddler's natural exuberance in readiness for a new day.

'Yes, my darling, you are very gorgeous too!'

Eden bounces up and down hard on the mattress in reply.

'Can I have some of your energy, baby girl?' Ashley asks and grins back at her daughter, but it turns into a wince as the pincer-pain grips her forehead. It's the first hangover she's had in a couple of years – since before she was pregnant. She groans.

'Oh, God. I have truly forgotten what this was like. I'm not sure that I have the energy to be Mum today…'

She rolls over in bed, turning away from her daughter for a moment. Though Eden can't possibly understand, something in Ashley doesn't want Eden to see her like this – the dregs of last night's makeup smeared across her face and staining the pillow, and her brain not quite functioning at full capacity.

Pull yourself together, she thinks. And then she notices the delicate flower, nestling on her pillow: a white orchid, given to her by Baz. 'It represents beauty and elegance,' he had whispered to her. 'Perfect for you.' She experiences a little tremor, an echo of the shiver that went through her last night as he said it.

And then she experiences another little jolt, remembering something that she read yesterday. She scrolls to check Christina's update.

Yes, there it is – *A flower will become significant.*

Oh yes, indeed. The white orchid. It gives her just the little fillip she needs. This is meant to be. It really is written in the stars. Ashley soon finds herself dragging her reluctant body from the bed and forcing herself to get up to fix breakfast for Eden. She wills herself not to look at her phone repeatedly, but in the end the temptation is too much for her. And there it is, already. A message from Baz. Her stomach does another little flip that has nothing to do with the hangover.

Morning Gorgeous. Really enjoyed last night. Did I dream you? Can't wait to see you again. B x

Yes. It all really happened and wasn't a figment of her imagination, and he likes her! She feels all the thrill of being a teenager again, embarking on an adventure, full of promise and excitement. So different from the recent drudgery and mundane routine of motherhood.

True, she conveniently didn't mention to Baz that she was a single mother with a toddler, stuck in a seventh-floor flat, but there was plenty of time to see how this panned out before getting into the finer details of her domestic arrangements.

Last night it had felt brilliant to just be like all the other girls in that club – young and carefree – if only for a few hours. A bit like Cinderella, she thinks, noticing Eden's fairy-tale book lying open on the floor. But I have no intention of letting my carriage turn into a pumpkin. I'm going to make this thing last, whatever it takes.

Christina's daily text pings in:

There's something different about you today. Everyone will notice your newfound radiance. You've set the wheels in motion for enormous change. Now that you have done the hard bit, sit back and let the rest happen.

Oh, she's so right again. How does she manage to do it? There's a lot in this psychic business. But wait, does that mean she shouldn't text Baz back? Before she can make up her mind, a second message flashes up from him.

So, can I tempt you back tonight for more of the same? I think we should get to know each other a little better. x

It's already happening, thinks Ashley. My luck is changing. My life *is* changing. She wants nothing more than to dance the night away with Baz again. Now, how to make that happen? Would Kerry babysit for a second night in a row? It's a pretty big ask – Friday *and* Saturday night. But why not? How long has it been since Ashley had a big weekend? Up until last night she hadn't been out properly in months. You can hardly call Nana's funeral going out. Kerry can have a night out whenever she likes. She isn't tied down by the responsibility of bringing up a child all by herself with no support network. She's a good friend. She'll understand how important this is.

Kerry's reply isn't as enthusiastic as the previous day's, but she agrees.

Alright babe, as it's you. Don't go making a habit of this, though!

Good old Kerry. Ashley's hangover seems to be lifting. She decides on a slightly teasing reply to Baz.

Might swing by later tonight – if u r lucky. A x

It's ever so much more nonchalant in tone than she feels inside, but she's determined to play it cool this time – to sit back and let it happen rather than forcing it. As Christina says, she's put the wheels in motion now. Baz can do the running. If this is her destiny, then it is meant to be.

She hesitates just a moment before hitting 'send', but once the flirty communication is done, Ashley switches her attention entirely to Eden, feeling just a little bit guilty about abandoning her last night. She does everything she can to make up for it and to make sure that they have a really good day together. It is a delight to be with her daughter. Eden: her name had been top of a shortlist of one when Ashley was choosing what to call her. Such a perfect little moniker for such a perfect little baby. Eden, from the biblical garden of Eden, meaning paradise or delight. And, while it hasn't always been exactly paradise bringing a child up by herself, they haven't done too badly, all things considered. Ashley relishes the time with her daughter today, especially since she knows that she is going to spend the night away from her again.

It is another brilliant night that goes by in a flash of retro glitter balls and disco lighting. And this time she uses the

VIP entrance, there is no need to stand in line. Baz must have briefed the doorman – who signals to Ashley to come forward and then ushers her straight on through. It is difficult to keep an eye on the clock, and it becomes another much later return than she promised Kerry. There is another 'free' taxi ride home. Another few lines of cocaine to liven things up. Another hangover to follow. But again, it is all worth it. And Baz is so attentive, such a gentleman. The VIP treatment didn't stop at the door. He wouldn't let her buy a drink all night. And, although he angled to be invited back to Ashley's, he didn't push it when she said she wasn't ready. She has had two of the best nights she has ever experienced, and they haven't cost her a penny. Ashley feels as if life is suddenly starting to *happen* to her. Just as Christina – and the newspaper horoscope – predicted it would. Destiny indeed.

Flirty text messages are exchanged all through the week, and the pattern repeats itself the following weekend, with two big clubbing nights, but Kerry is already fed up with being asked to babysit. She will do the Friday night if she really has to and Ashley can't find anyone else, but not the Saturday as well. She has end of key stage assessments to mark, and both weekend nights for two weekends in a row is a bit much: Kerry needs some weekend downtime, too. Ashley knows that she is pushing it by even asking, but she is desperate to see Baz, and makes the most of Friday night – surprised by how much she is loving getting back to the clubbing scene.

The problem of Saturday night looms over her. She simply has to go out on Saturday night as well. She *has* to. She still hasn't told Baz about the existence of Eden. The pumping music of the club isn't exactly conducive to cosy chats on awkward subjects.

She tries another friend to babysit for her. It's awkward to ask Dana out of the blue. She hasn't spoken to her for months – she's only stayed in contact with her by 'liking' the odd post here and there on Facebook.

To Ashley's relief, Dana agrees with very little persuasion. She doesn't have plans for Saturday night, so as long as it isn't too late, she will happily sit in Ashley's flat. Dana has only met Eden a couple of times – but Eden is a friendly, accommodating child, and it is all very straightforward. Dana arrives early so that she can be there while Eden goes to bed.

'She's a talkative little thing, isn't she?' Dana notices.

'Ah, it's cute, isn't it? Though most of it's baby babble nonsense. It's really amazing how much it sounds like a conversation. She's picking up real words and sounds all the time. She can do a few 'd' sounds – she might even be able to say your name!'

In the event, it comes out sounding more like 'Dada', and there is an awkward moment, which they both cover with a brusque laugh. Dana knew Matt from school, but doesn't like to ask about 'Dada', knowing only that they split up early into the pregnancy and that Eden doesn't see her father.

By the fifth weekend of partying, Ashley has well and truly exhausted all her babysitting options. Kerry is barely speaking to her, and Dana is suddenly 'busy' every time she is asked. There is a schoolgirl in the flat below who has offered, but she has to be home by midnight, which isn't really any good – that's just about when things start to get going of an evening. But not seeing Baz is not an option either. She has never felt like this about anyone before. Ever. Every day begins with a kind of fluttery excitement and anticipation. But it is more than that. Baz is central to it, but it is the whole scene at the club. The dancing and the drugs – which are completely under control, just a line here and a dab there to give her a little buzz – have brought back the meaning of fun to what was a fairly dull existence. And they also mean that Ashley is in great shape physically. For the first time in a few years, Ashley knows that she looks good. Really good. And looking good has kick-started the confidence that had been so lacking lately. If she's honest, since before Eden was born. She hasn't let her hair down – to use one of Nana's expressions – since Nana died. Maybe even since her mother died. It's time to live a little. Life is short.

Ashley has even stopped taking so much notice of Christina's daily messages and psychic updates, and no longer jumps to the horoscope pages online or in the magazines. A flower has indeed been very significant: Ashley glances at the orchid on the window ledge, but there is no need to rely on all of that any more.

The whole thing in some ways has actually made her a better mum, too – Ashley is certain of it. There are fewer hangovers now that she is getting back into the pace of the clubbing scene, and the inner confidence along with that outer glow has given her the spur she needed to try a few things. During the week everything is about Eden. She has baked fairy cakes with Eden standing by, allowing her to plunge her pudgy fingers into the mix and 'help'. They have undertaken some arty projects together; Ashley is rediscovering her creative side, as if she has a new energy source. And they leave the flat every single day now, Ashley makes sure of that. They head to the shops, to the park, even to the woods sometimes. The fresh air is doing them both good, and these days there is always a spring in Ashley's step as she pushes the stroller around.

Everyone has commented on Ashley's transformation. Her social circle has widened dramatically because of the club – and her elevated status that comes through being connected to Baz. Her Baz is the golden boy. There is a sense of pride, for Ashley, in his achievements. The White Orchid is a success, going from strength to strength. He has turned that place around in such a short space of time. Numbers on the door are up week on week. Ashley scrolls through the pictures from last weekend, noting with some satisfaction the perfection of her own new acrylic nails, paid for by Baz – a gift for helping him through these difficult first few weeks of opening.

She is young. She is single. But not free. There is Eden. Which brings Ashley right back to the babysitting problem.

Her phone pings with a message from Kerry. *Time for that catch up yet?*

Not if you can't babysit, Ashley thinks.

She has already half made the decision, allowing a previously subdued thought to rise to the surface.

Ashley is out of other options, so she considers the unconsiderable.

Eden is so good and sleeps so well that she never wakes up and *always sleeps through*. Ashley can't actually remember the last time she had to go to her in the night. It simply never happens. If she is only going to be out for a couple of hours – the club doesn't really get going until about 11 pm, and she can be back home by around three in the morning – what if she simply leaves Eden home alone?

The plan develops through the day, but Ashley realises that, if she is honest, she has been considering it for a few weeks now. Eden could be tucked into the wardrobe in the bedroom so that no harm can come to her (and the neighbours can't hear if she does wake up, which she won't).

The wardrobe is a large, old-fashioned thing that she inherited from Nana. It is made of dark wood, ornately carved into swirls and whorls – a really nice, solid piece of furniture, well crafted and much better quality than the Ikea stuff that the rest of the flat is kitted out in.

Ashley does the bedtime story with Eden inside the wardrobe, and manages to make a game of it, in fact. She fixes the little Upsy Daisy night light on a timer on a shelf inside the wardrobe so that Eden isn't going to sleep in the dark, places the cot mattress on the floor where it fits perfectly, and arranges all Eden's teddies around the edges so that it is soft and cosy inside – a cuddly little den. She also makes sure that she doesn't even start to get ready until Eden is long asleep inside – so that her daughter has no idea, won't even sense that her mum is heading out for the evening.

It is another fantastic night at the club, though Ashley is on edge the whole time. When the taxi drops her off in the early hours of the morning there is a slightly sickly feeling in the pit of Ashley's stomach because of Eden. What if anything has happened to her while she was gone?

She has nothing to worry about: inside the wardrobe, Eden is sleeping soundly, oblivious to all.

II

The conversation with Baz is much easier than she imagined it would be, when Ashley eventually plucks up the courage to have it. He isn't bothered at all about Ashley having a child already and being a single mum. Quite the opposite, in fact.

'That's cool – a ready-made family,' he answers, as if he is ready to become part of it.

Ashley experiences that lovely lurching in her stomach when he says it. They are curled up together on a makeshift bed in an upstairs room at the club.

'I know I was an idiot for not telling you before. I just thought that it might—' she pauses for a second – 'well, I suppose, that it might put you off me.'

'Nothing could do that,' he says, and with his arm around her neck he pulls her into him playfully. 'So, when can I meet her?'

'Soon, soon,' says Ashley, 'we'll definitely organise it. I wasn't sure at first, but over these last few weeks I've decided that I really quite like you,' she returns, equally playfully. 'But don't let it go to your head!'

'Listen, Ash. How about tonight? I could…' Now it is his turn to pause. He holds her gaze. 'I could stay over. If you wanted me to.'

The question hangs in the air for a moment.

'Oh.' Ashley wasn't expecting that; she isn't quite ready for it. 'Well… I'd love you to, stay over, I mean… but that's not the best way to meet her. What I mean is, she won't wake up and meet you tonight! It would have to be in the morning. She isn't even two years old, so you know, she tends to go to bed early,' she jokes, rather desperately. 'Anyway, in all seriousness, the flat's small – it's only a one-bedroom place. Not exactly the Ritz. It wouldn't be right for you and me, you know, with Eden there.'

Ashley kicks herself mentally. It's coming out all wrong. She's gabbling. It sounds as if she doesn't want him there.

'Ah, yes, right.'

There is an awkward pause for a moment.

It's Baz who breaks it. 'All the same, though. I'd like to get to know her. If you wanted me to.'

Of course she wants him to. And it's nice the way he doesn't probe too much into who and what and why. Or where Eden's father is. He hasn't quizzed her about any of it. He just seems to take it in his stride. Ashley has no desire to explain how things went wrong between her and Matt. How she had actually pushed him away and shut him out. How she was relieved when he left – telling her that he was too young for that kind of responsibility. How they were probably never right for each other anyway; being with Matt just didn't feel anything like how being with Baz does. Or how naive she was – and foolish to get pregnant in the first place. Or, in fact, how she has been organising childcare with the help of a large, obliging wardrobe. She doesn't have to say any of that to Baz. He just seems to take the situation at face value.

But when Baz speaks again a few minutes later, it is clear their thoughts have gone in a completely different direction.

'The thing is, Ash – I need to be honest with you now, too. I need somewhere to lie low for a bit. Things are heating up a bit at the club. Nothing serious, nothing either of us need to be worried about. Just that it would be better for everyone if I was off the radar for a couple of weeks. So, I guess I'm at your mercy. What's your sofa like?'

'The sofa! No chance. Think I'd let this body away from mine overnight if I knew you were in the next room?'

He smiles and looks directly at her once more. That lovely, forthright look that makes her want to do just about anything he says. She holds his stare, thinking.

'Well, maybe there *is* a way.' Ashley is hesitant, and she certainly won't explain it to him right now, but she has noticed that Eden seems to *like* being in the wardrobe at night. Almost to prefer it. She has got used to it over the last few months. It's like another room, anyway. It would be exactly like *being* in the next room, if the flat had one. A little mini perfectly Eden-sized bedroom – inside a wardrobe.

'That's my girl,' says Baz.

'We'll work it out. Of course you can stay. But, first you have to tell me what's going on at the club. Why do you need to get out of the way? Are you in trouble?'

'Of course I'm not in trouble! The boss couldn't be happier. Takings are up, the clientele are exactly the right sort, the Orchid is doing well. So, it's really nothing you need to worry that pretty little head about. I can't explain everything right now. Just – you know, the drugs don't grow on trees, so I've been dealing a bit. Nothing heavy, a little here and there. But I want to get out of that,' he adds, as Ashley's face registers concern. 'And I will. The club's making so much money that I don't need it any more, anyway. It would just be easier if I wasn't around after hours to get caught up in it all. You know what these people are like.'

'Yeah,' says Ashley, vaguely, even though she doesn't. 'Sounds sensible.'

'And anyway, wouldn't it be nice for us to be able to spend some proper time together?' He strokes her arm. 'Rather than snatched moments here?'

It would be *so* nice, thinks Ashley, mind nearly made up. How she would love to wake up next to Baz, rather than disappearing upstairs with him for a fumbling quickie before hastily redressing and going back down to the club. She allows herself to imagine him inside her flat, between her sheets, making coffee in the morning. She likes the picture. Could Baz really fit into that domestic role?

Christina had sent one of her psychic updates this morning:

Once again your world is about to change in a dramatic way. You are on the verge of a seismic shift. There will be upheaval and a period of readjustment. It is up to you to decide what you want and are prepared to sacrifice.

It had seemed cryptic when she had read it first thing. Now it seems prescient. Seismic shift, indeed.

'So I'll call a taxi, shall I?' He kisses her forehead. 'And this time I'll get in it with you. You don't know how long I've been waiting to do that. It's driven me mad waving you off each night and not being able to come with you.' He's gabbling now. 'I've got a few things packed in a bag here, just in case. I was hoping you would be up for it.' He has the mobile to his ear already, the number for the cab company on speed dial. As he makes the booking he grabs the zipped holdall with his free hand. 'Come on, let's head down, shall we?'

It all happens so fast, before she really has time to process what it is she has agreed to; within a few minutes they are back at her flat, Ashley fumbling for her key and making a warning finger to her lips.

As usual she is hit by a flooding sense of relief that the flat is calm and quiet – all is well. There is no sound of a crying toddler. Eden has not woken up in her absence.

'Nice place.' Baz nods his approval and places his holdall down by the sofa.

Ashley is pleased too that he has actually noticed. She *does* keep it nice. It's so small that she has to. 'Well, it's not much – but it's home.'

'No babysitter?'

Ashley thinks quickly, not willing to admit to her arrangement of abandoning Eden. 'Oh, Kerry – my mate – has just left. I texted her in the taxi to say we were on our way. We usually do that… to make less noise as we go in and out.'

'Fair enough.' As ever, Baz asks no questions. If he thinks there is anything odd about it, he doesn't say.

He removes a small paper wrap from his top pocket and, with a questioning eyebrow, begins to rack out a line for each of them on the coffee table. Ashley has never done anything like this inside the flat before. It has been a sanctuary for her – and Eden – a cocoon of safety from the real, outside world. Now it feels deliciously naughty, subversive, knowing that her daughter is just in the next room. But why not? Eden isn't watching. She wouldn't know what they were doing anyway, even if she saw. Ashley nods her assent and takes the rolled up note that she is offered, anticipating the hit – and the sex – that will follow.

'Coffee?' she asks, as the drug courses through them both.

He shakes his head. 'No. Just you. Come here.' He slips the thin straps of Ashley's top down her arms and begins to caress her neck. 'She's in the bedroom, is she? Then we'll do it here so we don't wake her.'

And Baz takes command, as he always does. After, they doze on the sofa in front of a box-set TV drama that Ashley struggles to engage with. There are too many characters to follow easily, and frequent outbursts of violence – gunshots mainly – that seem fairly arbitrary when she isn't following the dialogue. Instead she is lost in her own circular train of thought. *It is up to you to decide what you want and are prepared to sacrifice.* She isn't really sure what she is doing. On the one hand, it doesn't feel entirely right to have Baz here in the flat that is hers and Eden's. It has been just the two of them for so long. On the other hand, it feels bloody amazing to have Baz here in the flat – and doesn't she deserve to feel the way he makes her feel?

Beneath the blind she can see the little hazy glow of orange. She has no idea what time it is, but that light says it must be dawn. Eden will be awake soon. She feels wired. There is a scratchy feeling of barbed wire behind her eyelids. It's a long time since she's pulled an all-nighter. But she also feels *good*. On top of the world. Baz is here *in her flat*, she tells herself again. And he has packed a bag like he is going to stay. She begins to clear the detritus from the night before, restoring her flat to its customary order. There is nowhere to put Baz's holdall. It doesn't really fit here in the neat order of her sitting room. She slides it down the side of the sofa so that it is at least a little out of sight.

When Eden begins to murmur an hour or so later, waking from her slumber, Ashley surrenders to the idea that she isn't going to get any sleep at all. Deal with it. She moves Eden's high chair into the bedroom to feed her breakfast, careful to put a towel underneath it so that the bits of toast and lumps of Weetabix that Eden will inevitably drop won't ruin the creamy-white carpet. She doesn't want to wake Baz yet, and besides, sprawled across her sofa is not how she wants to introduce him to Eden for the first time. It should be special. She tiptoes past his now-sleeping form to the far corner where the kitchenette area of the room is. Not wanting Eden to hear the swearing or gunshots that still issue from the television, she turns it off, hoping that he won't notice. He doesn't stir at the ting of the microwave from warming Eden's milk, or the kettle boiling, or the opening and closing of the little fridge, or the pop of the toaster. He sleeps – well, like a baby.

While Eden is happily mashing bits of soggy toast into her face, Ashley clears space in a drawer in the bedroom, in case Baz feels like unpacking that bag later. He's not moving in, she knows that. What was it he said? He just needed to be off the radar for a few weeks. Having him here overnight still feels like a grown-up move: like taking the next step in their relationship, moving things on.

Still tiptoeing round, she slides the buggy out into the communal area in the hallway outside the flat, then returns for Eden, changing and dressing her as quickly and efficiently as she can with slightly shaking hands – as last night's drugs and alcohol make their way out of her system. The high chair will have to stay in the bedroom until later. Ashley wants nothing more than to cuddle up next to Baz on that sofa, forget about being a mum and just be left to suffer her hangover in peace, but it isn't an option. *I'm already making sacrifices*, she thinks. *Christina was right. She is always right.*

With Eden safely strapped into the pushchair and dutifully waiting outside, she scribbles a note to Baz and leaves it on the coffee table, now clear of any traces of white powder from last night. *Taken Eden to the park. Make yourself at home. Help yourself to whatever you want. A x*

In some ways it is quite nice being out this early in the morning. The park is empty apart from a few determined joggers. But there is also an air of unreality about everything. The morning light feels wrong – too harsh, as though it's judging her. The birdsong is loud but you can still hear traffic alongside it. The two things together seem really incongruous; Ashley has never noticed that before. She does a few laps of the park, letting Eden out of the buggy to have a go in the baby swing. She can toddle across to it by herself now, her pudgy, unsteady 20-month-old legs working hard beneath her. Standing behind the swing to push it, Ashley can snatch a surreptitious look at her mobile. Christina's message is already in. It is shorter than usual, and a little disconcerting.

The early bird catches the worm. Today's events will leave you in a spin. Make sure it's what you want and it isn't all happening too fast. Remember that you are in charge. Assert yourself.

33

Ashley doesn't like the note of warning that today's cosmic update suggests. Things *are* moving fast. And she also isn't sure about the other statements. What is that supposed to mean, 'the early bird catches the worm'? Surely it contradicts the idea of things happening too fast? It doesn't really make sense. Why does she need to be assertive? She likes what's happening to her – and she's never really been able to be assertive about anything anyway. Christine should know that. Perhaps it is all nonsense, as Kerry keeps telling her it is. But then Kerry doesn't know about the flower. In fact, Kerry doesn't know much at the moment. She slightly has the hump with Ashley for 'using' her for babysitting. Ashley knows that she is going to have to sort that out. Kerry is too good a friend to lose. She puts the phone away and switches her concentration back to Eden.

They are engrossed in swinging, Eden giggling delightedly on each gentle upward movement. She has started speaking much more in the last few weeks, beyond the baby-babbling – as well as some 'd' sounds, she seems to be focusing mostly on the letter 'm' at the moment and has three new, clear words. To Ashley's delight, one of them is 'Mama', and she takes every opportunity to make Eden say it. She has also learnt to say 'more', which comes out more as 'mo', but Ashley knows what she means; and a third 'm' word, 'man' – but she uses the first two together now, 'Mama, mo, mama mo,' to encourage Ashley to push her higher and faster on the swing. It is wonderful watching Eden develop her communication like this. She is able to let Ashley know so much more about what she wants – though 'more' is becoming problematic at mealtimes.

After a thrilled giggle at being pushed higher on the swing, Eden now has occasion to use her third word, as a figure comes towards them through the trees. 'Mama, man. Mama, man.' Eden points and, as Ashley turns to look in the direction of her finger, she is astonished to see Baz coming towards them, holding two styrofoam cups and waving a lollipop at Eden.

'Thought you could do with one of these,' he says, handing Ashley one of the steaming cups. 'To blow the cobwebs out.' He takes a nonchalant sip from his own coffee.

'You are amazing!' she says. 'How did you—?'

'And this must be Eden – who might just want one of *these*,' he says, cutting her off and presenting Eden with the lollipop, along with an elaborate bow.

Ashley swallows her nagging concern about the amount of sugar that Eden is consuming this early in the morning; and actually, it's irrelevant, because Eden is giggling again, and it is a lovely, thoughtful thing to have done.

'Now, now, Eden. You shouldn't take sweets from strangers,' she jokes, for Baz's benefit rather than Eden's, who is too young to know or be worried about stranger danger, yet. And it's Ashley's fault that they are still strangers after all, she thinks, before snuggling into the warmth of his jacket, and his body. It is so nice to be looked after. What an effort, to come and find them here at the park and bring coffee and sweets. What a gentleman.

'Introduce us, then!'

'Eden, meet Baz. Baz, this is Eden.'

'Hello Eden. Very nice to meet you at last. Let's not be strangers!' Baz stoops down and makes a show of shaking Eden's tiny, and now sticky, hand – almost as if they are sealing a bizarre business deal, thinks Ashley, and smiles.

They walk on further through the park, sipping coffee. Baz slips his free arm around her shoulders as she pushes on the buggy with one hand. Ashley wonders if it is possible to be any happier. She hadn't dared to dream that she might meet someone who would accept both her and Eden after it all ended so disastrously with Matt. And here is someone who seems willing to do just that. Somebody kind and generous and thoughtful. Until now she has never imagined being able to share that tiny little flat, or her life, with anyone other than Eden. It feels as though her life is being rewritten by a new author.

Baz interrupts her thoughts. 'So, like I said last night, I'm keen to stay out of the way of the club for a bit. Which means I have plenty of time on my hands for a change. It's a nice day. How about I take you two ladies out? I believe there's a fair arrived in town for the weekend – all set up on the old showground. Last day today. My treat.'

Ashley is almost too happy to speak. She might burst into tears if she opens her mouth and tries to reply. Baz, perhaps misinterpreting her silence, suddenly seems momentarily less sure of himself.

'I mean, only if you think that Eden would enjoy it. I know she's a bit young for the rides, but there's plenty to see.'

'Yes, she'd, I mean, we would – love that.'

'Good. Let's have breakfast first, though, eh?'

Baz treats her to breakfast in the cafe. Ashley can't remember the last time she had breakfast out, though it's more like brunch by the time they sit down. She can't face eating much; last night's cocaine has still stolen away her appetite and everything tastes of cardboard, but it is the thought that counts. And Eden happily munches on the bits of toast and sausage that are passed to her, babbling away in a world of her own, as delighted as Ashley with the change of scene and change of routine.

The fairground is quiet – a small early-Sunday-afternoon crowd made up mostly of families. Which is what they must look like to everyone else, Ashley realises with some delight. With Eden still so small they can't really do many of the rides, as Baz predicted, but they soak up the music and carnival atmosphere as they walk around the stalls. Ashley and Eden watch as Baz tries his hand at the coconut shy and at a darts challenge, winning a giant yellow Minion toy that he presents to a delighted Eden with a flourish.

'I'm not usually that lucky. Perhaps it's the good light helping me to find the target. I don't know if I've ever been to the fair in daylight,' Baz jokes. 'I didn't know what I was missing out on! Children are good for you, aren't they?'

They try to get Eden to say 'minion', and she manages as far as 'min-on', which makes them all laugh. Baz persuades Ashley to take Eden on the gentle 'teacup' ride and a mini merry-go-round made up of ladybirds. He stands by the buggy and takes photographs, waving exaggeratedly as they make each revolution. Is this really happening? Ashley can't believe how patient and attentive he is. She has a pang of doubt. Does she deserve it? Does she deserve *him*? She pushes it firmly aside. That is the old Ashley talking, the one who lacked confidence and stayed at home. Life is so much better now that she is less wary and reserved, and trying to be more sociable – as Christina's advice suggested just a few weeks ago.

When they get off the ride, Baz insists on candyfloss, in spite of Ashley's laughing protests. They laugh again at the face Eden pulls when the strange texture touches her tongue. Just as they are getting ready to leave, they bump into one of Baz's mates, Dev, who seems happy to stand by the pushchair for five minutes so that Baz and Ashley can go on the waltzer together. It feels like a proper 'date' when they hold hands to climb into the tilting car.

'Go for it, man,' Baz tells the ride operator, who sends them into a hectic, whirling spin that pins Ashley back in her seat. It is utterly exhilarating. She screams. They go so fast that she can no longer see Eden to wave, or tell which way is up.

When she gets off the ride, dizzy and disorientated with a fluttering stomach, Eden is crying.

'I think she was worried by you screaming,' Dev explains apologetically. 'I wasn't quite sure what to do. It's quite hard to explain that you're having fun when she sees you make that sort of noise!'

'Oh. Come here. It's alright, darling. Mummy's here. I wasn't hurt. It's okay.' Ashley lifts Eden from the buggy and hugs her tightly. 'Oh, you silly dumpling. Was that what you were worried about?'

To Baz, almost apologetically, she says, 'She's probably quite tired, too. All that stimulation. She's had a hell of a day.'

'Of course. I didn't think. You'll have to give me time to learn this stuff. I don't know what I'm doing with a toddler. Let's get her home.'

Did he just say 'home'? Is he really considering her place home after just one night on the sofa? Ashley is not quite sure how she feels about this, whether it is a good thing or a bad thing. On balance, she thinks it must be good – a measure of his commitment to their relationship, and how relaxed he feels around them both. He certainly seems concerned for Eden, which is a good sign. They head back towards the flat, just like any family returning from a day out. Baz takes over pushing the buggy, pretending to race the cars along the street, and then slowing down to link arms with Ashley when Eden tires of the game.

Still determined to keep entirely away from the club, he plans a quiet night in with a box set and a takeaway. 'You don't mind, do you?'

Ashley wonders if her day could be more perfect. Baz is just too good to be true.

Later, seeing the wardrobe arrangement in action for the first time, Baz isn't critical. He seems to approve. 'Oh, I see what you're doing there. Good idea. I like it. Almost as if you're sending her to her own private Narnia. Sweet. Space-saving,' and, 'So – does that mean I get to come to bed with you tonight instead of being stuck on the sofa?'

Ashley smiles, in what she hopes is a seductive way. 'Well, seeing as you've asked so nicely.'

When they fall into bed together a few hours later, Ashley makes sure to put music on, quietly, but enough to cover up the sounds of their lovemaking. Just in case Eden were to wake up and hear. Which she won't. Baz likes to play a little rough and it wouldn't do for Eden to sense any of that. Look how upset she got when Ashley was being thrown around on the waltzer.

III

On reflection, Ashley thinks, she most loves the *luxury* that comes as part of the Baz package. All the little extras that life with him brings. Being a single parent was tough financially. They never went without, she and Eden – Ashley was careful with the household budget, and savvy about what entitlements she had. There was a small inheritance from Nana that had enabled Ashley to get herself set up in the flat, paying a deposit and three months' rent upfront, so she would never go into arrears. But there has never been much spare for treats, and Ashley is cautious by nature. When it was just her and Eden, the flat was comfortable and they had everything they needed, but the budget didn't really extend to going out very much.

Things are so different now with Baz: there is money, and plenty of it. He is good at gifts and treats, and spoils both of them at every opportunity. He likes to surprise Ashley with meals out in nice restaurants. The kind of restaurants that Ashley hasn't been to before, that have white linen cloths on the tables and separate waiters for wine and food. The kind of restaurants where she doesn't know what to order because she isn't even sure what all the things on the menu are, so she just follows Baz's lead. He is always charming towards her, though sometimes she notices that he is slightly bullying towards the restaurant staff. It makes Ashley feel a little uncomfortable, and she also looks twice when her food comes out. She knows how petty kitchen and service staff can be in response to difficult customers, and wishes that Baz would be more careful when he speaks roughly, or condescendingly, to people when he really has very little cause to do so. She winced once, when he actually clicked his fingers to summon a waiter. When she was a student she worked for a short time as a kitchen hand in a pizza restaurant. If the chefs didn't like a customer for some reason, or a waitress they wanted to impress moaned about a customer, they put the ham in their armpit before they put it on the pizza. Out of sight of the customer, of course. The pizza would then be pushed through the big metal oven to be collected and delivered to the unsuspecting customer. Ashley wishes that Baz would be kinder to people. You never know quite what's lurking around the corner.

He is kind to Ashley, always. In fact, he has offered to pay for a babysitter when they go out, but there's no need: Eden is quite happy in her solid wooden sleeping space. And anyway, she still isn't really speaking to Kelly and there aren't that many other people to ask. Leaving her a couple of times a week has just become the norm. It is straightforward, and Ashley does it with far less guilt than she did in the beginning.

Her friends tell her how lucky she is. The ones who know, that is. She would like to be able to parade her good fortune for all to see, but Ashley can't play out her new life on Insta and Facebook because Baz refuses to be tagged on social media.

'Not cool, Ash. It's nothing to do with you; I just don't want certain people to be able to find me at the moment.'

She has updated her own status to 'in a relationship', which gives her a thrill every time she sees it written like that, but she has to make do with curating arty shots to represent it – an arm draped around her shoulder but no face to identify him. Two glasses of champagne and a cryptic allusion to her mysterious other half. A shot of their hands linked across a table.

Are you dating the Elephant Man? one wit quips in the comments beneath a selfie of Ashley facing the camera but looking over Baz's shoulder so that only half the back of his head is in the photo. *Why can't we see the boy wonder?*

Because I'm keeping him all to myself! She writes in reply. *Hands off!* The truth is she would love to be able to show Baz off more; he is as fit as anything – impossibly muscular and hipster good-looking, and nothing whatsoever like the Elephant Man. But it isn't the end of the world that she has to keep him to herself. It is a small price to pay, she tells herself, for the lovely life they are leading. Ashley has nothing to complain about. He is attentive, and does a bit around the flat when asked. He takes the bins out

– a job Ashley has always hated doing. And he pays for all their entertainment. Ashley never has to put her hand in her purse when they are out. There's probably something old-fashioned about that, but it feels quite sweet. And anyway, he doesn't pay towards the housekeeping. It's like a kind of unwritten contract that she will keep the household running and he will sort their leisure expenses – take care of the 'fun' in its various forms.

Presents and surprises and little treats come regularly. The flat is always filled with flowers, and Ashley now has a growing collection of jewellery. Her favourite piece is a simple gold chain that she wears almost constantly. The jewellery always arrives in expensive-looking packaging, and Ashley ignores any nagging question she might have about its provenance, or how Baz has managed to afford it on his income from the club. Baz is vague, anyway, if she does probe.

'Enjoy, Ash. Yours is not to reason why.'

It's an odd expression; it sounds like a quotation, perhaps, but she takes it at face value and doesn't question further.

More importantly, as far as Ashley is concerned, Baz is making plans to celebrate Eden's second birthday with a trip to a local farm park and a catered party. Eden has never had anything like that before, and she doesn't really have many 'friends' to invite along, but Ashley really appreciates the effort that Baz makes with her. And actually, he is really quite good with her, given that by his own admission he's never really been around children before.

One of the things she appreciates the most is that he has still never quizzed Ashley about Eden's father, or even made reference to the previous relationships in her life; he seems to understand that it is a private part of her history that doesn't belong to him and is none of his business. For that, Ashley is always very grateful. It doesn't occur to her that Baz is not interested enough – she reads it as giving her space, treating her as an adult. She is still not ready to talk about Matt and her own immaturity and mistakes of the past – though she refuses to think of Eden as a 'mistake' in spite of the fact that she never intended to get pregnant.

So, on balance, Baz has been amazing for her, and for Eden, which is the important thing. Things really changed the night she met him. Ashley now feels as though perhaps her life means something, finally, in the way that other people's lives do – the ones with jobs and careers and degrees and purpose, the busy strangers that she used to watch from her seventh-storey window, and the ones that she knows, those who have begun their own businesses, or made their way up several rungs of the career ladder. In the past she has envied Kerry her teaching career and admired the time she spent struggling towards a dream. Not that Ashley wanted to be a teacher; she couldn't imagine herself in a role like that, nor has she ever known that kind of drive towards anything. When she looks back now, she sees that she rather drifted through school and assumed that a dream would find her at some stage.

She did just enough to get five decent GCSEs, but could never be described as a student who distinguished herself academically.

There were good reasons for that.

Nana had never pushed her to achieve, and the teachers left her alone to get on with things in her own way. A dead mother was a handy way of making you exempt from homework, apparently.

It wasn't that Ashley ever really got into trouble at school – she never took emotional advantage of her status as an orphan, living with her grandmother. She was a quiet student whose main aim was to not stand out. She lacked the confidence to do so anyway. She didn't like being singled out because of her tragic past; it became second nature to try and blend in. That way she made herself into one of those students who it would be easy to overlook.

When friends began making plans for future careers it only caused her mild anxiety. Experiencing the tragedy of losing your mum so young was supposed to make a person stronger, more resilient. Something would turn up. She just didn't expect it to be a baby, the thing that defined her. But Ashley is proud of the way she has brought up Eden on her own. She never even tried to settle down with Matt. There was nothing between them – they both agreed that. Matt would stay out of the way. They were both too young for this. No point in messing up two lives. Her own mother had managed without a man, and so would she. She was used to women bringing up women. That was how it worked in her family, her Nana stepping in when her mother's life was cut short.

But now there is a man. There is Baz. And life has more meaning and direction than it did before.

Baz is one of the least judgemental people she has ever met. He just accepts Ashley at face value, and doesn't question her decisions or routines or probe into her past. In fact, the only thing he does pass comment on one morning is her small, but very specific, book collection, arranged in height order on a little shelf in the bedroom.

'Quite a little library you've got there, Ash.'

'Thank you.' Ashley takes it as a compliment, even though she suspects that it probably isn't intended as one.

'Christ, you're really into this stuff, aren't you?' He has a copy of *Decoding the Stars: Your Guide to Unlocking Astral Secrets* in his hands, but there are also books on palmistry and tarot cards alongside the extensive zodiac and horoscope-related volumes.

'Well... I think it's important to understand your destiny,' she answers, feeling the need to defend herself against some kind of implied criticism.

'Right. So, can you read tarot cards?'

'I'm learning. I can't do it properly yet – not without referencing what I'm doing the whole time. I'd like to be able to, though. It's interesting.'

'Fair enough.' Baz pauses for a moment. 'Do you want to read mine?'

Ashley thinks for a moment. 'Not yet. Nice to keep some surprises in store, don't you think?'

He nuzzles into her neck and puts the book down. 'Oh yes, I like surprises. I've got one for you now,' he breathes as his fingers reach for her under the bedcovers.

'Not in the morning, Eden might be awake already and hear something,' she reminds him.

'It won't take long...' his hands are very persuasive. It makes for a very pleasant start to the day.

Baz's smooth transition into their lives is not without its problems, though. For one thing, it is exhausting playing the roles of 'mum' and 'party girl' 24-7. They don't sit very comfortably alongside each other. There are too many drugs, and while she doesn't mind it when they are out at the club – it's just part of the scene – it seems to be creeping into the flat more and more. Baz's time of 'lying low' is over and he is back working at the club full-time, but he prefers the peace and quiet of being at the flat, he tells her. Because he is at the flat pretty much all the time during the day, it feels as though they never have any time apart. He treats the flat like home. Which is nice on the one hand – good that he can feel relaxed enough to do that. But on the other hand, it's beginning to feel a little claustrophobic. It's partly that Ashley had no idea how much she has grown to value her own space and her own company. She finds herself taking Eden out of the flat more and more during the daytime. It's not that she's being pushed out, exactly. More that she needs air – and snatches of time away from Baz.

Their relationship, in particular their sex life, is intense. Ashley knows that she's not devoting the time and attention to Eden that she once was. There isn't space and time to do it in quite the same way as before Baz came along. And she can't relax in the bedroom. She feels uncomfortable with Eden there in the wardrobe, even though Eden can't see anything through the thick, wooden doors – which can't be opened from the inside; Ashley has checked. Still, there is just something a bit strange, a bit unnatural about it. Ashley has never really been happy with having Baz here indefinitely. What was an emergency solution has become a permanent arrangement.

Baz has very specific tastes. He likes her to do things that sometimes seem a bit full-on. And sometimes he likes to film it. Them. Her. And Ashley isn't confident enough to speak up to explain that she isn't comfortable with some of it. Most of the time she is out of it by the time they reach the bedroom anyway, but there is a residual feeling of wrongness the next day when she thinks back to what she has done just a few feet away from her daughter.

The drugs thing is bothering her more and more. Not whatever Baz was up to, or perhaps still is, but the partying inside the flat. Ashley knows that she doesn't think right when she isn't straight. Thoughts mess with her head, and in that muddle she knows she's not always in control of situations and decisions. She has played music too loud, too late. She has let things get out of hand with people coming back to the flat at times. Too many people, too late at night. Her neighbours have even complained about the comings and goings and what a change seems to have come over Ashley.

She's tried to raise it with Baz, but he always smooths things over.

'You're not worried about what other people think, are you? Look. Whatever happens, I'll look after you. You know that, don't you? You and Eden, you're the most precious thing that's ever happened to me. Whatever goes on with me, and the club, you're not involved in anything. Remember that.'

It's chivalrous, the way he keeps her out of it. Chivalrous rather than patronising, Ashley tells herself.

The most important thing, though, is that Eden doesn't seem to be affected by it so far, as far as Ashley can tell. But it's difficult *to* tell because Eden never makes any noise inside that wardrobe. She's never been one for making much noise, never really been one for much crying, even when she was tiny. Everyone's always commented on how good she is, meaning 'quiet'. Whenever Ashley opens the wardrobe to go and get her in the morning, she is always just there, awake. Sometimes standing up, sometimes sitting down; never asleep but always quiet. There aren't any outward signs of Eden being upset. Sometimes Eden's face does look a little smudged, as if she has been crying. But she never hears anything and Ashley tells herself that's ridiculous.

Babies can't cry silently. Adults can. Heaven knows Ashley cried enough silent tears when she first found out she was pregnant, then breaking up with Matt, and after, when Nana was dying. That was the worst time, when Ashley realised that she was all alone in the world and contemplated just what a colossal mess she'd gone and made of everything in her life. But not babies. Not toddlers. Not two-year-olds. They couldn't be capable of crying silently. Ashley hoped not, anyway.

It would be too sad to bear.

IV

Baz has been living with them for a couple of months when he suggests a different kind of evening out.

'Greyhound racing, Ash. You're going to love it. There's a nice restaurant at the track and it will make a change from our usual spots. My treat.'

Ashley isn't at all sure that she's going to love it. She thinks there might be some cruelty involved in that kind of sport, if you can call it sport – or at least exploitation of the dogs, trained to chase in a circle after a hare that isn't even real. And aren't there problems in the industry about what to do with the retired dogs? And saying 'my treat' is unnecessary. It's always his treat.

'Look. I bought a copy of the *Racing Post*. It shows you all the dogs and their recent form so you can choose which ones you want to bet on.'

Ah, yes. Gambling. There's that side to it, too. Ashley doesn't really like the sound of that either. It all seems a little bit pointless. Too risky and dangerous. A way of throwing all your money away for no good reason.

But Ashley puts her concerns to one side and allows herself to be carried along on the tide of Baz's enthusiasm. She doesn't want to appear ungrateful. He shows her what all the different numbers and abbreviations on the page mean, why weight might be important, how each animal has performed in its last few outings. Ashley decides that the names of the dogs are more interesting, and that is how she will pick out which ones she'll choose in each race.

She gets Eden ready for bed as usual. And Eden, as usual, makes no protest about being put inside the wardrobe. It might be Ashley's imagination, but Eden seems quieter lately. She seems to have stopped experimenting with new words. It was only a few weeks ago that Ashley felt as though she couldn't keep up with all the new language Eden was learning. Now she's not sure that she has heard a new word for a few days. And a few times she has not used a word that Ashley is sure she has already learnt almost as if she is regressing a little in her speech. Eden is very quiet at bedtime; perhaps she senses that they are going out without her and is sulking.

'We'll be back before you know it, darling,' Ashley whispers. It's difficult to gauge quite how much Eden understands these days. She has probably heard all the talk about the racing and realises that she is not being included. That will explain her grumpiness. Ashley has a pang of guilt as she turns the key in the wardrobe lock just before they leave. The dog track is a little out of town, a little further away than they usually go from the flat.

'Perhaps we should ask Nina to babysit?' she suggests, hurriedly.

'A bit late now, isn't it? We need to leave or we'll miss the first race. Eden will be fine. She always is, isn't she? What's the difference tonight?'

There is none, Ashley thinks. Eden doesn't know how far away things are, so it makes no difference if they are in the restaurant up the road or the one at the dog track 45 minutes away. Ashley just feels happier when she is close by, but it feels a bit lame explaining that.

With a large glass of wine in her hand, wide-eyed at the novelty of the greyhound track, Ashley is soon caught up in the buzz of excitement and expectation at the races. Baz bumps into people he knows, and although Ashley is always introduced, she is never really part of the conversations, so she has plenty of time to observe what is going on around her. It's quite a 'male' environment. There is plenty of handshaking and backslapping and words that she doesn't understand. She recognises a couple of the men who are gathered near Baz. Dev, who was at the funfair with them a couple of months back, gives her a friendly smile of recognition but doesn't say anything. Lachie, Baz's boss at the club, looks her up and down appraisingly. before turning away from her and chatting to the man next to him, someone in a flashy suit who Ashley isn't familiar with. Without even making eye contact he has managed to make her feel uncomfortable, to signal that she is somehow beneath the bother of saying 'hello'. She is already starting to feel a little bit out of place. She doesn't understand the chat. And there is a great deal of cash about, she notices. People, including Baz, seem to be carrying wads of it.

'Here's a fiver, Ash. Go down and put something on at the Tote for the first race. I'm going down to where the bookies are, trackside. I'll meet you there in a sec.' He points out of the window down to where the independent bookmakers have set up their pitches. A row of men in similar large camel-coloured wool coats or raincoats and various different hats (some favouring a flat cap, others with dark Fedoras) all stand in groups of two or three next to boards displaying more bewildering numbers. They look so bizarre as they go through the motions of their secret communication signalling system, touching their wrists or upper arms, or even ears, in their uniform of Big Coats. Baz tried to explain some of the terms to her this afternoon. She knows that 'pony' and 'monkey' are references to sums of money, but they are meaningless to her. The jargon makes her feel excluded. Baz also explained that bookmakers talk in a combination of 'tic-tac' hand gestures, some rhyming slang and some other disguised words, so they have developed their own language for communicating with each other in order that their customers, the 'punters', will not understand what they are saying. The dog in trap one is referred to as 'eno' or 'tops'; Ashley can see some sense in that, but the trap two dog is known as 'bottle', which she doesn't understand at all. It means that anyone listening can't easily be party to that inside information about the greyhounds and where the money is going. To Ashley it just looks like the Big Coats are talking in playground secret code.

She has already decided on the name of the dog she is going to bet on in the first race, but isn't sure whether to feel affronted or grateful to Baz for giving her 'pocket money' to spend. Still, she's happy not to be throwing her own money away, she realises. Before she puts the money on, she looks again at Christine's psychic update for today. A message which ends unequivocally, *Today is not a day to take a gamble*. She knows that the word 'gamble' here is likely being used figuratively, and probably not as in 'whatever you do, don't put a bet on', but still, she is so attuned to trying to take the advice that she is offered from the various astrological perspectives she has come to rely on that she has to think twice before slapping her money down on the counter. She has no idea about forecasts and reverse forecasts and trios and feels entirely out of her depth.

'Garden of Eden,' she says, uncertainly.

'Is that each way, love, or to win?'

'To win,' Ashley answers, a little more definitely.

A piece of paper is handed back to her that says 'Garden of Eden' on it. Ashley likes seeing Eden's name – it feels more like she is here with her, rather than left home alone in a wardrobe.

She heads down the steps to find Baz. It is a clear evening but chilly outside, and she shivers, seeing now why the bookies wear the big coats. She scans the throng of activity in front of her, but there is no obvious sign of Baz.

She finds herself next to Dev. Now that they are apart from the testosterone-fuelled group upstairs he seems happier to talk to her.

'Hi Ashley. It's good to see you. How are you? How are you finding things?'

Ashley finds herself feeling touched that he has bothered to remember her name.

'Good, good. Yeah. You?'

'Yeah, not bad.'

He glances down towards the piece of paper that Ashley is clutching. 'Have you got a bet on in the first?'

'Garden of Eden. I couldn't resist.'

'Oh yes – Eden. That's the name of your little girl, isn't it?'

She's touched that he has remembered that, too. She smiles and nods.

'I don't want to burst your bubble, but I'm not sure that 'Garden of Eden' has much of a chance in this one, I'm afraid. It's quite long odds. The favourite's in trap three.'

'Yeah, well, you know – I just liked the name. It's all good fun – but some of it's a bit bewildering to a newcomer like me. It's my first time at the races.'

At that moment Ashley can't help herself from giggling at a rather portly Big Coat who has been furiously shouting 'hold up the bottom' down the line to his bookmaking colleagues. It probably means something very important, but frankly it sounds a little bit silly.

'What's funny?'

She isn't sure she wants to admit to her ignorance too freely to Dev, who she hardly knows, but he's being very nice to her.

'Just the stuff they say. Like "hold up the bottom". It just sounds strange.'

'I suppose it does. It means that they should probably stop taking bets on trap six, or at least be wary of laying it. There may have suddenly been a substantial bet on that dog. They're worried that some of the punters know something they don't.'

Two minutes to the off, the announcer says over the stadium tannoy system. The action in front of each pitch increases with this news of the approach of race time – and starts to feel frenetic as the dogs are going into the traps. Ashley finds herself caught up in the wave of excitement. There is lots more shouting and jostling as punters try and place their bets, invariably left to the last possible moment. Most of the shouting is by the bookmakers. Now she sees Baz, handing over what looks like a parcel, rather than notes, to one of the Big Coats in the middle of the line. Strange. The Big Coat doesn't break stride in his complicated hand gestures as he slips the package into the inside lining of his coat.

Dev sees her looking, sees that she has seen whatever transaction has just taken place.

'Listen, Ashley, it's not really my place to say this, only—'

'Yes?'

But whatever Dev was about to say to her, he seems to hesitate and change his mind as Baz comes towards them.

'Just be careful, yeah?'

Be careful? Of what? thinks Ashley.

The hare is running, the course commentator announces, and the moment is lost as Baz reaches them.

'Good luck,' says Dev. Somehow Ashley thinks that he is talking about more than just the race.

There is another palpable change in atmosphere. Suddenly all eyes are focused on the track as the dogs are released from their traps. The air itself sharpens up. It is all over in what feels like a few seconds with a giant, collective roar from the crowd as the dogs pass the finish line just in front of them. It is a blur of fur and colour. Ashley has to look up at the screen nearby to realise that Garden of Eden has come home last.

Baz showers her with more £5 and £10 notes through the rest of the evening. Ashley decides just to keep them rather than throw the money away. Christine's advice is probably right. Gambling is going to get her nowhere.

And what was Dev trying to warn her about?

V

There is a loud hammering, like something is knocking right through Ashley's skull, breaching her defences while she lies sleeping. *That must have been some night*, she thinks, groggily, nearing consciousness, and assuming a hangover. She puts her hand to her head to try to stop it, before she realises that the hammering is real and not inside her head. It takes a few more seconds for Ashley to realise that there is someone at the front door. Someone angry and insistent, pounding away at the wood relentlessly – no ordinary knocking. It is still dark in the bedroom, no light coming in through the curtains. There is shouting, loud and threatening-sounding, but she can't make out the actual words. Not just someone, several people, different voices. Who could want to come in at this time of the night? Are these the drug-dealing people who Baz was so frightened of? Or something worse? It feels as if she is having some sort of nightmare. What has he done? What the hell has he done?

'Fuck, fuck, fuck,' screams Baz, leaping from the bed and hopping from foot to foot as he tries to get one leg into his trousers. His 'fucks' punctuate the air in rhythm with the battering, until all at once both stop with a splintering shatter. There is a moment of silence before pounding feet find their way into the flat. In another second they are in the bedroom.

'What's going on, Baz?' Ashley hears herself yell, before throwing herself towards the wardrobe instinctively. *Must protect Eden.* Before she reaches the door there are men in the room. Men in dark clothes reaching for Baz and for her. Men in uniform. Oh shit. She knows what's going on here. She's answered her own question. Her fears are confirmed seconds later.

'Barry Gainer, I am arresting you on suspicion of drug-related offences. You do not have to say anything, but it may harm your defence if you do not mention when questioned something which you later may rely on in court. Anything you do say may be given in evidence.'

The handcuffs snap around Baz's wrists.

No, no. This is what happens on television, not in real life. They can't be here in her flat, in her bedroom.

'Tell the fuckers nothing, Ash. Do you hear me?'

'Stand back from there, miss. We need to do a thorough search of the property.'

'But I haven't done anything—'

'Christ, there's a kid in the wardrobe.'

'EDEN!' Ashley screeches, but it's too late to do anything. Arms are reaching into the wardrobe for Eden, and they're not hers.

Ashley is naked and only now realises the indignity of this; her first thought had been for Eden. The police officer who said the words that make it sound as though they are in an episode of *The Bill* hands her a shirt to put around herself, for which she is grateful.

Everything happens very fast, and yet Ashley experiences a moment of stillness and a moment of clarity amidst the chaos. Whatever is going on here, whatever this mess is, this is not who she is. She isn't about dawn raids and drugs busts and splintering doors and violent, forced entry into her home. What does she really know of Baz? This man who is being dragged from her bedroom. How has she let all of this into her life? She realises that she is not concerned for Baz's safety, but for Eden's and for her own.

With Baz gone, the police officers are kinder. They give her time to get herself and Eden dressed and to pack some food for Eden. They apologise for upsetting Eden – they hadn't expected her to be inside the room.

She calms Eden, makes them coffee. Contemplates more. Baz may have punctured their paradise for now, but it won't happen in the future. Ashley is determined not to be beholden to a man again. What was she thinking? This is one surprise she has definitely not enjoyed. She has a strange feeling of wanting to rewind time. But when to? Does she really wish she had never met Baz? It's really difficult to assess her feelings for him in this moment. She feels a loyalty towards him, but is also experiencing a sense of betrayal.

Her determination to distance herself from Baz only increases when she finds herself at the police station, separated from Eden temporarily, being questioned. She is not under suspicion herself, she is told, but helping the police with their enquiries. Baz, it turns out, is suspected of all sorts of things beyond the drug-related charges.

'Were you aware of Mr Gainer's involvement in filming and distributing porn?'

It is a female police officer firing the questions at her, and she has a kind of mock-sympathetic voice that Ashley doesn't quite trust.

Distributing porn? He has filmed Ashley doing all sorts of things to him, and he to her, but for them, not for distribution. What is this?

'No. Porn – absolutely not. Look, I'm really nothing to do with this. Baz was just staying over. We haven't known each other all that long...When can I see Eden?'

'Soon. She's perfectly safe. She's being looked after by a social worker until we get to the bottom of what's going on here. Your boyfriend has been a *very* naughty boy. We need to determine what your role was in all of this is. What do you know about the brothels that Mr Gainer was running?'

'Brothels?'

'Have you ever been to 247 Stanley Street? Do you know that house? Do you know what goes on there?'

'No. I don't. I don't know anything. I don't even know where Stanley Street is. No clue what you're talking about. None of

this makes sense. I have nothing to do with Baz's work or…
that. But I'm sure he hasn't done anything that bad.'

Ashley is not actually sure of this at all. Police officers
don't break your door down in the small hours of the morning
for no reason. She has the strangest feeling of wanting to put
her hands over her ears and just block all this nonsense out.
She's tired and fed up with being asked questions. Unfair
questions that she shouldn't be made to answer.

'Anyway, are you going to pay for my door?' she finds
herself saying. Fear is making Ashley uncharacteristically
bold. 'That wasn't Baz's door, you know, it was mine. That
was my home you smashed into this morning.' She is surprising herself by the words that are coming from her mouth.
She is not her usually meek and mild self.

The police officer makes notes in the file in front of her.
'Don't worry. That will all be taken care of.'

'What are you writing down? I'm the victim here. Can't
you see that? I shouldn't be here at all. It's Baz that's under
arrest, not me. Where's Eden? Where is she? Is she here at
the police station? I need to see her. Are you even listening to
me? I NEED to see my daughter.'

In fact, a little bit of knowledge is a dangerous thing.
Ashley does know a little bit more than she is letting on. If
she is honest with herself, she has had an inkling over the
last few months that not everything that Baz says is entirely
truthful. The night at the dog track has shown her that Baz is
still involved in 'underhand' activities. She has caught wind

of one or two disturbing things when she has been at the club. She should have been firmer with him. But she does believe that Baz hasn't done anything really bad because – and she doesn't tell the police officer this, it's Baz's mess, he can sort it out – what he has let on is that he is taking some of the heat off his property-developer boss, Lachie, the owner at the club. Lachie who, according to Baz, is the real villain of the piece. Baz is just being paid by him in order to redirect attention away from some of Lachie's less palatable activities. Or at least, that's what Baz has told her. She doesn't, thankfully, know enough to tell the police anything very much, so she isn't lying as such. And the last thing Baz said was to say nothing – not that he deserves her loyalty after what he has put her through.

Ashley's phone pings. It seems to echo unnaturally loudly in this small, uncomfortable room. She glances over at it. The police officer opposite her nods, as if granting her permission to read it. Ashley, after all, as she has already pointed out, is not under arrest herself. She is merely helping the police with their enquiries. Voluntarily. As a good citizen. The alert heralds the daily text from Christine. Talk about timing. She can only see the start of the message.

There will be some significant upheaval today…

She's not wrong.

The police officer is as good as her word, and after the interview Ashley is brought to Eden, who is quite happy, playing with some toys at a family centre nearby, being looked after by a family liaison officer. She doesn't seem traumatised or confused by the fact that she has essentially witnessed an arrest, that strange people have been in her house, that there has been shouting and, to use Christine's words, 'significant upheaval'. Leaflets are thrust into Ashley's hands explaining how best to handle the situation, how to talk to her child.

The liaison officer is smiley and supportive. 'Eden's had a lovely time here this morning. Don't worry about that. But you need to take special care in the coming days. A sudden disappearance without explanation can leave a child confused and scared, as they can often sense when something has happened. A child who is not told where their um, relative, is…'

'Baz isn't a relative,' Ashley cuts her off.

'Right. Even so, he's been a presence in your home. An important one, I assume. And therefore a significant presence in her life, even if only for a short space of time. Do you mind me asking how long you have been with your partner?'

Ashley thinks back. The last months have been a blur, really.

'Not even a year. Nine – maybe ten months?'

'Well, it may not sound like a long time in the grand scheme of things, but that's more than a quarter of Eden's life. Young as she is, she may worry about him and what has happened, and imagine things which may be much worse than the reality. This might be especially true when the adults around her are upset or angry. Children often internalise their feelings which can result in nightmares, tantrums and withdrawal from others. Don't be surprised if you see a change in Eden's behaviour over the next few days.'

Ashley can only nod. If she speaks now she will burst into tears. After her anger back there in the interview room, she is now ready to crumble. What the hell has she got herself into with Baz? How dare he do this to her and Eden? Things are going to change. Baz brought this on himself, and however guilty or not guilty of any crime he is, he is certainly guilty of bringing this chaos and ugliness into their lives. How could she have let that happen? Ashley is so cross with herself. And him. And frightened. Suddenly her legs give way and she is being directed towards a soft chair as the nice liaison officer hands her a tissue.

Baz is quickly sentenced to 10 months in prison. An age. Longer even than the entire time Ashley has known him. After sentencing, before he is taken away, he is able to return to the flat briefly, at a prearranged time. Ashley, cowardly, makes sure that she is out when he is due to be there. She doesn't want to see him.

It's already lonely without Baz. And boring. She misses him. Life is back to a mundane routine of childcare and staying in. But she is better off without him. Boring is better than violent dawn raids. She almost can't believe that it actually happened. It still feels like she was watching some terrible TV drama. How much her life has changed in what she now realises was actually such a short space of time.

Now she can sort the flat out properly. She can begin to get their lives back on a safer, healthier track. She can spend more time with Eden. Focus on what's important. She hasn't been fair on Eden recently. She definitely doesn't want to have anything more to do with Baz. He has not been good for them, in spite of the money and the treats. It hurts her, but she was never comfortable with the lifestyle he had been gradually luring her into. She has no intention of going anywhere near the club.

She thinks back ruefully to the days when she thought that Baz was too good to be true. It turns out that he was. She spends time scrolling through Christina's messages that once seemed so prescient. She sees now how they could be read in two very different ways. She notes the warning tone that she ignored. She remembers when Baz asked her to read his cards. Perhaps she should have done. She might have had a chance to get out before disaster struck, if she could have seen what lay ahead. Too many regrets.

Within a couple of weeks the flat is clean again. Ashley has scrubbed it from top to bottom in an effort to erase the months of memories, as if to eradicate the time they spent together. The orchid he gave to her that first night is thrown out. It had begun to lose its blossom anyway and was looking scraggly and unkempt. The rest of his stuff is packed up into the holdall and stored at the top of the wardrobe. Eden's wardrobe. It is the only thing left.

All other traces of him are gone. She puts a blanket in front of the holdall so that she can't see it and be reminded of him whenever she opens the wardrobe, where Eden continues to sleep. She can't *quite* bring herself to throw Baz's things away. She just needs to stop thinking about him. She has agreed with the social worker that it is best if they have no contact while he is in prison. She is making a fresh, new start, as if the last 10 months haven't happened.

So Ashley is entirely unprepared for the knock at the door one evening when Eden is safely down for the night.

The chain on the new, reinforced door is in place as always, and Ashley peeps through the door viewer first. She has felt a constant fear and anxiety inside her home ever since the horrible morning of Baz's arrest, as though it isn't safe inside any more. She feels the same way as she did when her mother's home was burgled when Ashley was much younger. It is a different place, somehow, even though it is located within the same four walls. She has thought about moving, and has got herself onto the council house waiting list, hoping that she might qualify for a two-bedroom apartment, or even a little house to give them more space. It would be great to have a garden. And Eden will qualify for some free nursery hours soon, so she could even start to work, or study.

She gasps. She had hoped for Kerry, maybe; a friendly face checking up on her. But Kerry has distanced herself since the arrest – as a school teacher, she doesn't want to be connected in any way with the wrong side of the law.

But it is a man in a smart suit standing on her doormat outside the flat. A man she recognises, but doesn't know well. One of the last people she might have expected to see turning up at her home.

Lachie.

Baz's boss: the owner of the club. The big boss, the money man. An important man in Baz's world, but a man who has barely given her the time of day, beyond the briefest of acknowledgements any time she has been at the White Orchid. He certainly hasn't been in touch since Baz went inside. What on earth does he want with her? She draws back the bolt and removes the chain.

'Ash-ley,' he says, drawing out her name as though they are long-lost friends. 'How are you, babe?'

Ashley stands entirely still for a moment. Dumbfounded. Lachie is absolutely one of the last people she expected to see, and she is completely thrown off guard by his presence.

He takes the moment to appraise her – casting his eyes up and down over her body. 'Well, now. Aren't you going to let me in? There's a good girl.' He flashes her a big, wide toothy smile. The grinning teeth of the wolf.

Ashley steps back to let him pass.

The wolf, once inside her home, is smooth. 'It must have been truly awful for you. I can't imagine. But don't worry.' He sits down on the sofa and pats the space next to him – as though it is his home and he is welcoming her in, instead of the other way round. 'You've been very brave. I'm not going to leave you out in the cold while my boy is...' Here he pauses for a moment, choosing the right word. 'Away.'

He places a little packet, wrapped up, down on the coffee table, and next to it a pile of notes – several hundred pounds in used twenties. 'Here. I thought this might help. It's all for you, my dear. There's plenty more where that came from. You just shout out when you need it. I promised Baz that I'd take good care of you, and see you right while he's not here.'

That big, flashy smile again. 'And I am a man of my word.'

Ashley doesn't trust him an inch. But he is edging towards the door before she has a chance to respond.

'Anything you need, you just let me know. Anything at all,' he calls from the hallway, letting himself out of the flat.

There is nothing Ashley could possibly need from this man, is there? Though he hasn't laid a finger on her, she feels as if his oily voice has coated her in its poison. She fingers the drugs he has left her. Finances have been much trickier since Baz went. There is nothing much left in the fridge. The last thing she wants to do is deprive Eden. She has no more money until the end of the month. She has no other means of support, no one else to help her out. The notes will come in very useful. He has been generous.

It isn't until the second visit, a few days later, that Lachie makes his real move on her.

'Now that we understand each other a bit better, I have a little proposition for you. You've been good for the club – good for Baz. Now it's time to step it up a little. Your duty – while he's inside.'

Ashley notices that there is no delicate pause about where Baz is, this time. He is 'inside', not merely 'away'.

'Do you know what I mean?'

Ashley shakes her head, though she is starting to guess before he spells it out for her.

'You've got to keep things going. You've got work to do if you want to keep young – Eden – that's her name, right? Keep young Eden in the style to which she has been accustomed.'

Ashley shivers when he says Eden's name. How dare he? But she makes no reply.

'And you're my little insurance policy for while Baz is inside. It won't take much – no more than a few hours a week.'

Every fibre of her being wants to scream at him, 'Get out! Get away from me. Get out of my flat! I don't need you!'

But she doesn't. Those words don't come. They don't form because of the threat that falls from his mouth next.

'Because, well – we wouldn't want any harm to come to young Eden, would we?' Lachie licks his lips.

And all of a sudden there is no fight left inside Ashley. She will do anything to keep Eden safe.

'What do you need me to do?' she whispers, hating herself.

'This and that. Things that a woman of your looks and talent will find very easy.'

Ashley doesn't like the sound of 'this and that'. Nor the way that Lachie brushes her cheek when he talks about her looks. 'Easy? To do what?'

'Come on, Ashley. You're a woman of the world. I know you are. Baz has told me. You just need to make yourself available to some of my important clients. Simple as that.'

Ashley shivers. The emphasis on 'available' is unmistakeable, and yet Lachie somehow makes it sound so innocent and straightforward.

Quite why certain clients are 'important' and require this treatment, Ashley never finds out. But she does as she is bidden. She doesn't really feel as if she has a choice. Eden is left alone more and more in the evenings, often until very late at night when Ashley returns. Sometimes Lachie comes back with her to the flat – escorts her for a nightcap. Often more than a nightcap, and sometimes with more of his 'clients'. Drugs and alcohol make it all bearable, especially when Lachie becomes increasingly controlling – both in terms of supplying the drugs and in relation to what Ashley is asked to do. Ashley finds herself being pushed closer and closer to the edge as she is encouraged by Lachie to have sex – in front of him – with the other men that he chooses.

Lachie makes no secret of the fact that Baz is simply taking his 'turn' inside, being paid off to serve the crimes of his boss, and Ashley isn't sure quite at what point she realises that Baz, for his part, did a good job of grooming her for this role. By the time she works it out it is too late: she is in too deep to find a way out of the mess around her life.

By the time that Baz comes out from his first stint in prison six months later, Ashley barely registers his return. Somewhere between Baz's arrest and Lachie's fateful knock on the door a few nights after, she has lost her way entirely. Baz was the catalyst for the catastrophe that has overtaken her life, but Lachie is the true culprit for the calamities that follow.

Soon, Ashley begins working for Lachie full-time in the brothel, and loses her flat, becoming resident at 247 Stanley Street, an address she once denied all knowledge of. Gone are the days when she could claim not knowing about Lachie's various enterprises. Now she knows all too well. She has unwittingly become part of Lachie's sex ring, alongside a number of other vulnerable women, some of whom, like Ashley, have children. The wardrobe is moved to 247 Stanley Street, and the cycle of Eden being locked inside continues while Ashley 'works'.

Ashley no longer controls, nor has the energy to care about, what happens to her own body. She is degraded and abused until she no longer knows who she really is.

Meanwhile Eden grows bigger, sleeps less, and hears more from her tiny wooden vantage point. Sometimes the door is locked, sometimes it isn't.

One night she pushes open the door, eyes wide with concern for her mother.

Lachie is often there, looking on, as he is on this particular occasion. He hears that little creak. He sees those saucepan eyes looking out from the darkness inside. He can't have Eden interrupting. That wouldn't do at all. He finds a way to make sure that Eden stays quiet.

Even though Lachie is a father himself, he never displays a moment's concern for the frightened little Eden.

Quite the opposite, in fact.

Part Two

Louise

Chapter 1

'Ayyy hayyy! Oh, yeah, baby!'

The sun is shining and I am belting out 'Baby, here I am, signed, sealed, delivered, I'm yours!' at the top of my voice with some percussion on the steering wheel and a few improvised 'mmm-mmm's in the style of Stevie Wonder for good measure. To be fair, Stevie is probably slightly more tuneful than I am, but the radio is turned up loud, the car is bringing me home, and the world feels like a good place to be right now.

I still have a few miles to go to reach my own front door, having just said a teary goodbye to a little lad who has been staying with us. I am on my way back from dropping Daniel off at his mum's house. It has been a wonderful and emotional few weeks. Sandra, Daniel's mum, has just come out of hospital following a big touch-and-go operation as part of her cancer treatment. Daniel came into care with us while she was away because they only have each other – he had nowhere else to go.

I really enjoy this kind of respite care. And on this occasion it has been a real joy to have him with us in the house. Although he was, of course, anxious about the outcome of the operation, the early prognosis is good. He and his mum are very close, and Daniel didn't come with any of the usual baggage that placements often bring – just good manners and an innate delight about everything around him. He was so charming and grateful that he has managed to teach us all a thing or two about counting our blessings and knowing what we should be thankful for. Of course, I have the usual sadness; goodbyes with our little foster children are always sad. No, that's not true – they are *nearly* always sad – sometimes it is a relief when certain children, who clearly need more help and specialist intervention than I can give them, move on. I don't like admitting to that feeling of relief, but it's definitely part of the general 'background noise' of foster care.

But that little bit of natural goodbye sadness is replaced by the uplifting feelings I have in this case: it has been simply heart-warming to see Daniel reunited with his mother, and although we will miss this endearing young man, I just feel glad to have been able to help out. This has been a win-win situation, as some might say, and I can sit back and enjoy the feel-good factor, because it doesn't always feel like this.

'You got my future in your hands,' I sing, still engrossed in my own private karaoke session, which is why I don't notice my phone ringing. I don't hear it and I can't see it, as it is slung into a corner of the empty passenger seat so recently vacated by Daniel, and masked by a bottle of water rolling about.

I stop at traffic lights and glance over to see the missed call. It is Daria, our current supervising social worker, and she has left a text message as well as a voicemail, so she clearly wants to talk to me. I pull over just after the traffic lights. I know that everything is alright with Daniel – I've just seen him off – so what's the problem?

It is another placement referral. Of course it is. What else? A little girl aged five years old. Wow. That really is super quick. Daria, although a locum, already knows that I always like a short break between placements if I can. 'We'll have a little break, I'll catch up with my work, the children can regroup and the dust can settle,' is what I usually say. The children mime along to the words as I say it, I've said it so often, but they know as well as I do that it rarely happens in practice. There is such a shortage of foster carers that in reality our services are constantly required. It would be easy to be left feeling used and undervalued, but the trouble is, something inside me has already lit up at the thought of opening the doors and welcoming a little five-year-old person into our home, even as I'm giving myself a good talking to, telling myself off and wondering if I will ever learn.

I get a few more details before I make any promises. Daria is a recent arrival from Romania, who has followed her dentist husband to the UK to find work. We haven't known each other very long, but I get on well with her. She is a lovely person, full of warmth and empathy. In Romania, I have come to learn that they practise a much 'kinder' form of social work than we seem to here. I was surprised by this as, perhaps fuelled by media reports, I have a perception of Romania as a country of hardship and despair. I have vague memories of hearing about Romanian orphanages years ago, and I guess the notion has remained with me as a misguided and ill-informed hangover from that era. I do know, though, that Daria has struggled with some of the approaches to social work she has encountered here at times. Her frank manner leaves me in no doubt as to what she feels about certain procedures and practices. For now, she is very happy to explain in her near-perfect and very precise English about the prospective placement.

Eden – a pretty name that I am immediately struck by – is currently being looked after by a foster carer who I know, and am admittedly not very fond of. Daria mentions her name. Daria doesn't say it, of course – she's too professional to be critical – but rumour has it that Janey, the foster carer in question, has a note on the front of her file to say 'only use if no alternative available'. I don't know if it's true or not, but I can imagine that it should be. Janey and I were once at an event together for looked-after children, when I witnessed her grab the arm of a little boy she was with and drag him away roughly. This disturbing image has stayed with me for several years and clouded my judgement about my 'fellow' foster carer. Given the number of professionals who were also at the event, I was quite stunned that she wasn't challenged at the time – but perhaps the note on the file is a reflection of her behaviour back then.

Apparently, this little girl, Eden, is on a fold-up bed in a room with two other children – none of them are siblings.

'So, you see, Louise, it is not the ideal situation for a little one.'

When I first began fostering, many years ago now, we were told that children shouldn't share rooms and should have their own proper single bed: no doubles, fold-ups or futons. I understand perfectly about having a room to themselves. It is hard enough to be inside someone else's home without having a quiet space to retreat to when you need. Ironically, nearly every child I have fostered has asked for a double bed. If we go on holiday and they get the chance to sleep in one, they love it. So I don't understand the thinking there in relation to a double bed, but having a 'proper' bed certainly makes sense. If you are being fostered, then life is likely chaotic enough without further suggestion of improvisation and impermanence. So I agree with Daria: this doesn't sound ideal for Eden. I wonder how she has ended up there in the first place. I have noticed that social workers and managers can bend and change the rules depending on the situation – perhaps that is what happened in this case when they were looking for Eden's initial placement.

Daria tells me more, and my heart goes out to this child and her mother. Yet another young single mum caught up in a situation that has spiralled out of control. Involved with the wrong bloke, low self-esteem: the usual stuff. Eden's mum is receiving some therapeutic support while she remains in prison serving out her sentence. I'm not allowed to know the precise details, of course. But she is serving a term of two years, so Sherlock Allen here deduces that it isn't murder.

The child is described as 'quiet'. I know that this means much more than that. As a foster carer you soon learn the language used in referrals. 'Lively' is an interesting and especially euphemistic one: I have looked after several children who were described as that and their behaviour was off the wall. I don't suppose that 'Unable to sit still for five seconds and climbs the wall like Spiderman on speed' fits easily into a box on a form. 'Energetic' is another one I dread seeing, for similar reasons. You learn to infer a great deal from the different adjectives that are never casual, but always carefully chosen descriptors. Each one is loaded with so much more than it might be in the 'real' world.

Sometimes there can be a photograph of a child, but that usually only happens if they are going to be put up for adoption. This has always baffled me, as it's the same child whether fostered or adopted; sometimes a foster placement will convert into a long-term arrangement, maybe move to special guardianship or even adoption – but for some reason the social workers think that seeing a photo of a child will influence the decision of the foster carer to the child's detriment. It's all a bit mad really. I would love to have been able to see a photo of Eden right now. That way she becomes real, a person in her own right.

So what else can I learn about quiet little Eden?

Her health seems okay – so clearly her mum cared about that and did right by her. That's a good start. Life can be complicated, and a long time ago I learnt to try not to judge or begin blaming the parents for things they may simply have no control over. Stuff happens to all of us. This is a weird world we live in, so I try to form a picture of their lives while avoiding making those judgements – which is much harder than it sounds, because we make them naturally all the time. There is one caveat to this, and that is when a child has been sexually abused. I know then that I am in dangerous territory, because I do begin to judge. I can't help myself. It makes my blood boil, but I also know that it isn't always that straightforward. To 'desire' a child has to be right up there with the other clinical illnesses, and should therefore be treated medically; but it also, to my mind, has to be dealt with punitively. I am, however, learning and adjusting all the time. Thankfully, there's no evidence of that here.

I'm sold. Now I just need to see how the rest of the family feel. I get back on the road and cover the last few miles, Stevie keeping me company all the way.

I wait until my husband, Lloyd, and the children are all in the kitchen, grabbing plates and sitting down around the large wooden table – a table that I realise is now over 30 years old. I brought it back from Guildford tied to the top of my Fiat Uno. It had been a display table for chinaware and was already scratched, hence its bargain price. I liked it because it was dirt cheap and had a personality. It came from a branch of Habitat which was closing down. I still love it. It has even more of a personality these days. Scratches have become etchings, each one telling a story. It has heard an awful lot of conversations, witnessed some dramatic scenes, played its part in a number of lives, this table. It's probably a good thing that it can't talk.

I also realise, when I look down at the brown bowl I am mixing the salad in, that this too has a long history with my household; it was bought from a charity shop when I was a student. Time flies, the people here change, but my kitchen props stay the same. Perhaps it is time for another change.

I put it to them. 'So. A little girl called Eden, aged five, needs somewhere to go.' There isn't an answer straight away. I carry on tossing a salad that is now well and truly mixed, but I don't want to interrupt the rhythm or disturb the moment. I can see from their faces that they are processing my statement, all working out how a five-year-old is going to impact on their lives.

Vincent, now seriously into his gaming, is in such a routine of his private online world that not much can permeate it. He's the first to say, 'Yes. Don't see why not.'

Jackson loves younger children and nods his assent alongside his brother.

Lily, my long-term foster child, chews it over for a little while longer. 'Well. She *must* keep away from my teddies, but – yes,' she finally decides, satisfied with that proviso.

Lloyd asks to read the referral before committing. 'I'm not saying no, obviously. I just want to have a look first.'

I don't blame him. He knows what I am like, and he also knows realistically from past experience what our family can reasonably commit to. He asks a few questions, but this one looks relatively straightforward. If having a mother in prison can be deemed straightforward.

I leave everyone to help themselves while I phone Daria back.

'Thanks, Louise. Actually, someone else has come forward, so I'll check what's going on and get back to you.'

Oh no. I hate it when a placement becomes competitive. It feels like it turns into an episode of *Location, Location, Location*. Or should that be *Placement, Placement, Placement*. We resume our evening, but my thoughts are consumed by Eden. We don't have to wait more than a couple of hours.

'Yes, she's all yours. The others, they didn't like the idea of taking her for contact in prison. So she will be better off with you.'

Strange. The prison details were clearly marked on the file. Of course contact would take place there. And I see this kind of thing as part of the challenge of fostering. It's certainly never dull. I make a very small, celebratory fist. We won. Pathetic, I know. The trouble is, whenever I receive a referral like this, I am always mentally settling the child into the Allen home way before anything has been agreed. I don't like to have the rug pulled away from under me!

'She will come to you tomorrow.'

I feel the usual shiver of nervous anticipation. But mostly I am excited. Here we go.

Tomorrow, a new chapter begins. In Eden's life and in ours.

Chapter 2

I didn't want to tempt fate before we were sure, but now I can get to work. The room that Daniel was staying in is perfect for a little girl called Eden. Or at least it will be in a minute, when I am done with it.

I strip the bed, open the windows, trot downstairs and hang the duvet over the line to air along with the pillows. I move all the furniture away from the walls and hoover behind and underneath. I mop the sea-blue painted floorboards. I drag out one of the spare wardrobes from behind the corner of the stairwell and select some small, brightly coloured coat hangers from the drawer in the guest room to fill it. I guess that if she is coming from Jancy's she will have the standard black bin-bag of clothes, the ubiquitous badge of the child in care. I dust the remaining surfaces in the room, humming a little, entirely happy in my labours. Next I go to my beauti-fully ordered linen cupboard, currently scented with bars of expensive soap. They were given to me by a friend – a rash purchase from Lush that was no longer wanted – but I am an extremely grateful recipient, luxuriating in the fresh fragrances that permeate the shelves and give my linen a lovely smell. I select a cheerfully patterned bedding set with a pink sheet and make up the bed. The room is bright, fresh and clean, but I'm not quite finished.

I spend most of the evening arranging and perfecting Eden's new room; it gives me great pleasure to create a tiny bit of order for a new arrival. However much reading and preparation I do from the child's file, I can never know quite where they come from or what their lives were like before. I would never presume that their mums and dads didn't give them the best they could, and I need to match that. For reasons that I can't really explain I already have a warm feeling about Ashley, Eden's mother. I think (and hope) that she has thus far been a good mum. She won't be the first to have ended up on the wrong life path when it comes to lifestyles and caring for children. Life is complicated, and circumstances get beyond all of us at times. Avoiding judgement is the first step for a foster carer. Blame and judgement – and their partner, despair – do nothing to make a child feel good about themselves, or help them to settle in somewhere new.

I am old enough now to be the age of the mothers of some of the *parents* whose children have been taken into care. I'm probably more like the age of Eden's grandmother than her mother; my stepdaughters may well be a similar age to Ashley. I think back to when my stepdaughters were young and reflect on the myriad ways they brushed up against danger and bad choices. It was by luck as much as anything that they made it through some difficult times – and ended up eventually on positive life paths. It would be nice to think that decent parenting played a role. Certainly, as a foster carer, my parenting life has been scrutinised over and over by successive social workers. My parenting skills have been put under the microscope time and time again. It isn't easy. We all get things wrong. I have sympathy for Ashley, whatever it is that she may have done to wind up in prison. But I have a gut feeling about little Eden: I feel that she has been loved. Let's see.

As ever, I have no idea what possessions Eden will bring with her, but I am guessing that it won't be a lot. It never is. Children in care learn to travel light – often by virtue of where they have come from – and by the necessity of the reality that they are going to.

I put a few books and an ornament or two on her shelf – enough so that it doesn't look empty, not enough to be overwhelming. If she is here long enough she will fill the shelves with her own, self-chosen things. But the room still looks a little empty. I drag in a yellow wicker ottoman – she can use it for clothes or for toys later on, but it adds more colour to the space. I learnt at the beginning that making up a children's 'dream bedroom' from my misguided perception of what they might like according to my own taste and personality, however much fun, is actually ridiculously inappropriate. For a child in care, sometimes less is more. Too much 'stuff' isn't good, though it can be very tempting to provide it. They can feel smothered by it, or imposed upon – inserted into a life that isn't their own, when they already lack control and agency over so many things.

I remember this very clearly with Lily when she first arrived with us. She now has a beautiful room. I mean, we argue regularly and repeatedly about its tidiness, but that's normal and healthy and I am not going to worry about that. But when she came initially she systematically rejected nearly everything I had bought for her. Her taste was quite different from mine and her birth family did things differently from us. I quickly learnt that I must not thrust our family's ways onto a child, but include their habits and tastes and, wherever possible, allow them the luxury of choice.

Lily had shocking table manners at the start. From the beginning I did work on this, carefully and incrementally. I explained why elbows shouldn't be on the table and why her mouth needed to be closed when she ate her food. I explained that it is part of my job to help children become wonderful adults who can live and work with other people, who will be trusted to do important tasks, and be a pleasure to be around, because their manners are good enough.

I did tell a desperate lie once, which I am ashamed of now. I said out loud that she would earn more money and have more life chances if she knew her manners. Experience has taught me much about the prisms through which we view people. Back when I was teaching at the university I had a different view; I watched one of our pro vice-chancellors eat like a pig, and I also had an ex-boyfriend who had attended one of the most expensive schools in the land who had no manners at all. No manners on educated people looks like arrogance. On poor people it looks like ignorance. To my mind, it is that simple. Perhaps that's what I meant, or was trying to avoid, when I told my white lie to Lily.

I muse on all of this as I fall asleep, happy with my preparations for Eden's arrival.

Morning brings with it the usual chaos and, once the children have dressed, breakfasted, made plenty of noise, wound each other up, rushed back in for whatever it is they have forgotten, and finally departed for school, I have a chance to check my emails. I have to remember that fostering is just one amongst many things that I do, balancing it with my other roles. It's not my only job; it's a sad fact that I would have to be very wealthy for that to be the case. My career is in art, and now in books. I have writing and illustrations and painting to do, all of which hinge upon commissions and meeting deadlines.

Currently, I'm involved in setting up a project to get art to looked-after children. I have seen that these children – who carry their trauma around with them like an oversized backpack – need an outlet that isn't smoking, drink, drugs, sex and crime. We need to show our traumatised children other ways of seeing the world, to help them find avenues for self-expression and understanding, and art is a great medium through which to do that. It was certainly an important outlet for me as a young person, long before it became a career. But the setup of this sort of project takes a good deal of time, networking and organisation. I dedicate a little time to forwarding the cause. Eden, like any new placement, will take up plenty of my time, especially at the start.

I'm busy drafting some additional aspects of the project proposal when Eden's social worker telephones to give me the vague arrival time of 'around lunchtime'. Her name is Helen and she sounds nice enough, but gives nothing away over the phone.

I finish my tasks early, dispensing with them all as efficiently as I can but without my usual attention. I have other things on my mind this morning, and find it difficult to settle to them properly once her arrival has been confirmed.

I sit in the kitchen looking at the large clock, deliberately resisting the compulsion to undertake all the obsessive cleaning and arranging activities that come to mind. Perhaps I could reorganise a cutlery drawer, or re-sort all the tins in the cupboard. The minutes tick round interminably slowly. There must be glue on that minute hand. I still have at least an hour to go until Helen gets here, and time is moving through treacle. Instead of cleaning and clearing, I find a copy of *Elle Decoration* and spend a little while flicking through the glossy pages, dreaming about a new interior for the house. Wouldn't it be wonderful to afford all these beautiful objects, I sigh to myself, reimagining first the kitchen, then the sitting room and the hallways. Then I remember that actually I have a house full of children and teenagers – and dogs – and smile to myself; the reality could and would not be the picture I see in the pages of the magazine. And that is the way I have chosen things to be. The magazine goes back into the rack. But I can't settle. I find myself putting everything away off the draining board until there's not even a teaspoon left. Every surface in the room is clear of clutter. If you had ever visited, you would know that's not like me at all. I even find myself rearranging fridge magnets on the front of the refrigerator. What on earth for? What has come over me?

Eventually, after what feels like several millennia, but is actually just after 12.20 pm, the doorbell goes. It makes me jump slightly, even though it's the sound that I have been waiting for. I dash out into the hallway to open the front door, not wanting Eden to be left standing outside it a minute longer than she has to. I am surprised to see, through the coloured Victorian glass in the door, *two* adult silhouettes alongside the child-sized one. I wasn't expecting that. I'm curious as to why a little girl needs a bouncer alongside the social worker. It's not unprecedented; I have had this with sullen teenage boys in the past, who are heralded as trouble-makers and arrive with something of an entourage – but then, as soon as the 'guards' have gone, are delightful. Never before have I seen it with a child as young as Eden. Strange.

I throw open the door and deliberately look straight at Eden first – before acknowledging the adults – and smile. She is the epitome of a gorgeous child – light brown hair curling gently round a pale face – greeny-blue eyes peering up at me with a slightly pensive expression, reinforced by puffed-out cheeks. She doesn't say anything in response to my smiling 'hello', but seems very shy, and hangs back slightly. All behaviour which is only to be expected, and makes her even more endearing at this first meeting. It must be impossibly hard to arrive at the home of a stranger and know that you are going to be left there.

Helen announces herself on the doorstep, and again seems quite nice, if a little on the young side – but, as I have to keep telling myself, that is more likely me getting older than the social workers getting younger. She doesn't introduce me to her colleague as yet.

To break the ice I say to the two adults, 'Expecting trouble?' and laugh loudly at my own joke, but neither seem to notice my attempt at humour and it falls flat.

I invite the party inside the house as efficiently as I can. There is always that awkward moment as people are invited into a home they have never been to before – who goes first, and how it is managed in a narrow hallway.

'Just go on past me and through,' I usher cheerfully. 'I'll close the door behind you.'

Eden walks past clutching a tatty old teddy, faded and threadbare. Her grip suggests that it must be an important teddy, and I resolve straight away not to wash it. Not yet, anyway. It is likely that it has everything she needs to help her feel safe oozing from its fluffy grey pores.

Her colleague is eventually introduced as 'the social worker's assistant'. These people seem to be called something different every few years: team workers, support workers, business support and so on. But there is still no explanation of why she might be here.

We all go into the kitchen, me bringing up the rear as I wait to close the door behind them. 'That's it. This way.' Then, having given everyone a moment to establish themselves in the room, I follow that up with, 'So, what would we all like to drink?'

'You first, Eden,' I say cheerfully. 'What would you like? Would you prefer a soft drink? Maybe some diet cola?' I nod encouragingly, studiously ignoring Helen's raised, judgemental eyebrow. I'm not perfect; if water was the only choice available it would not be exciting for the children – it is rare that they ask for it as a first 'real' choice. Of course, I ration the fizzy or sugary drinks, but I find offering it at the start sends a little signal: it tells new children that we are not stuffy and uptight, but sensible – most of the time. They can have fun here.

Eden does not look at me directly, but softly shakes her head and holds her teddy a little closer.

'That's okay, Eden. Maybe you would like something in a moment. Let me know if you change your mind. What's your teddy called? He looks like a nice chap!'

She doesn't respond, other than to pull teddy a little tighter into her chest. I don't blame her. It's the only thing she knows right now in this place.

My kitchen is large, but now it seems filled with people. I gesture to everyone to sit and we arrange ourselves around the table. Eden sits in one of the painted chairs. Interestingly (to me) she chooses to sit in the teal blue chair, not the pink or red as so many other children do. She has chosen what I perceive to be the more sophisticated colour, and I am immediately intrigued. Good.

I empty a packet of biscuits out onto a plate: cookies with hazelnuts. Out of the corner of my eye I watch Eden study the plate, while I continue making friendly chit-chat with the two social workers. Without making any eye contact or even moving my head, I gently nudge the plate towards Eden. It is a silent gesture of encouragement. I'm deliberately not looking at her, and perhaps less deliberately nor are the two women. After a moment's hesitation, she responds. I notice a little hand dart up and, in silence, with a snakelike stealth and precision, take a biscuit from the plate. The hand is quickly placed back in her lap. Again, I think, *Good*. It is a start. She waits another moment, to make sure no one is watching perhaps, then Eden slowly raises her hand up to her mouth for a quick nibble, before returning the biscuit back to her lap. I smile – to myself – but in a way that I hope is also reassuring to Eden.

Helen wants to talk *about* Eden directly of course, and I am never comfortable with this – especially in these important, opening moments of arrival. It's such a strange dynamic. Here we are in Eden's new home. The child in this situation, no matter how old they are, has to sit and listen to their life and behaviours being described and dissected, without ownership of that narrative. Occasionally they are asked a question, usually something cringe-worthy or patronising. I really do feel for children in these moments. It's always awkward and it leads me to interrupt the meeting very strategically, before Helen can go any further with her line of conversation.

'Eden, would you like to go into the garden room, which is through the kitchen door, just here?' I open it to show her. 'There are toys in there, pretend cats and dogs to play with, and the real ones will be along in a minute.' I don't think I can keep Dotty and Douglas out in the garden any longer; they are desperate to meet Eden, too. I can hear them scratching at the door.

Eden is delighted with this idea and we walk through together. I fill a plastic cup up with water – I know she said she didn't want anything, but I suspect politeness and shyness have dictated her answer – and take the plate of biscuits into the garden room with us. Biscuits, as I know from plenty of experience, can make you thirsty. The garden room is large, light and airy and is what it sounds like: a bridge to the outdoor spaces of the house. The roof and sides are almost entirely made of glass, and consequently there is a different quality of light from the rest of the house. Large plants vie with garden implements for space in the piled-up corners. A stripy woven hammock hangs from the ceiling;

behind it is some gym equipment – currently unpopular and seldom used, but who knows when there will be a sudden fitness revival? There is a rolled-up yoga mat, buckets of toys, balls, hockey sticks, beanbags, a skipping rope, stacks of swimming towels, discarded flip-flops – even a giant metal duck, an old fairground mascot who has taken up residence there and who we somewhat unoriginally called 'Donald', before rechristening him Hueydeweylouie.

Eden edges around towards the box of toys and begins to sort and rummage. Unfamiliar toys are always a potential treasure trove.

'That's it – you see what you can find while I bring the dogs through.' I leave her to it; she can see us from where she is. I am far happier with this more distanced arrangement: she is occupied with something, and not the centre of attention on a difficult day of change and upheaval.

I release the hounds, which is a rather grand way of saying that two very small Chihuahua-Jack Russell crosses are finally allowed in to clatter claws across the creamy flagstones and welcome the new arrival. Suddenly there is a blur of fur and girl and tails.

'That's Douglas,' I say, pointing to the one who flies towards her first. 'And Dotty is…' My introductions come late. They hurl their tiny bodies at Eden, who busies herself making a fuss of them in return. They are already making friends, and Eden is a whole new centre of attention – but one that I suspect is much more fun, and will hopefully enable her to feel less pressured and more relaxed. That will keep them all occupied for a bit.

The social workers smile as all this takes place, but they are cool smiles and I wonder if they are a little annoyed with me. Perhaps they have detected an implicit criticism in my removal of Eden. I'm not bothered. I stand my ground and say nothing. This is my home and I am doing my best to be a good, welcoming host to the one who matters most right now: Eden.

Helen and 'Terry' (I finally learn her name after she has been in my house for a good 10 minutes) sit and drink their coffee whilst running through the paperwork: the various forms that need to be filled and boxes that need to be ticked. I have plenty of questions and first ask the documented ones about Eden's health and her education plan; I then follow up with the more personal ones: what she likes to eat, for example. Little is forthcoming in return. They don't seem to know the answers to either the big questions or the little ones. But when I look at Eden I see a healthy, well-developed child. I conclude that she hasn't been neglected in terms of health in the long term. She looks fine, a little thin, maybe, but not in any way worryingly so, and children can drop weight quickly. Upheavals such as the ones that she has just been through can easily lead to a temporary loss of appetite. But there is something: the permanent red rings around her eyes that I noticed straight away. It's as though someone has drawn a blunt red pencil through her eyelashes, and this fascinates me. Has something caused it? Is it just part of her physiology? Lloyd has perpetual dark circles around his eyes and when he hasn't shaved he looks disturbingly like a face on a wanted poster.

After the paperwork and my continued resistance to talk about Eden's mum within earshot, I suggest we all go and see Eden's new room.

'Are there any bags that need to go up with us?' Now that I say it, I don't remember seeing either of them holding anything on the way in. 'Does Eden have something in the car that you want to bring up?'

They shake their heads in unison and Helen, at least, has the decency to cast her eyes downwards. That toy box is going to be pretty empty for the time being. And the wardrobe is evidently redundant.

I raise my eyebrows. 'Does Eden have a budget to buy new clothes?' I whisper, as quietly as I can.

'There is, but no more than £100 for everything,' Helen whispers back.

Good start. Not. I know from experience that trying to claim this back could be very slow. It occurs to me that Daria, my supervising social worker, has not arrived yet. Although we have spoken regularly on the telephone, we are yet to meet in person and my two guests haven't met her either. In her role as a locum she has only been working with the authority for a few weeks.

Just as we all begin to walk up the stairs, there is a knock at the door. I dash to it and see a dark-haired woman in stunning bohemian clothes; she has olive skin, like me. I realise that I am inadvertently admiring her because she looks a bit like me; growing up in care myself has left a residue of an identity crisis, and an innate curiosity about people. She looks as nice as she sounds.

But, just like that, poor Eden is now surrounded by four adult women, three of whom she has never met before and a fourth, Helen, who she has only known for a short time. All here about her, making decisions on her behalf. It's tough on a young kid, it really is.

I say hello to Daria, and invite her inside to join the conga heading up the stairs. I explain what we are doing to Eden as we file up together. As well as all the adults, the dogs follow along too, taking advantage of the reality that I won't do my 'gruff voice' to tell them off when we have visitors.

Eden's room is the one with its door wide open. Experience has taught me to do a quick recce before a social worker visit, and make sure everything is in order in the areas they will see. I have been round already to close all the doors of the rooms they do not need to go into – in the interests of self-preservation. They only ever need to see the rooms that the foster child will be using; anything else feels like an impertinence. If they ask to see more – which happens sometimes – then I think they are being nosy. My home is just that – *mine* and *home* – and it is not up for inspection. It sometimes seems as if the authorities see the homes of foster carers as an extension of their workplace, over which they have jurisdiction. There is nothing to hide, but I like to hang on to my privacy as much as possible.

I take the time to gently observe Eden as she moves through what will become her home – and resist my usual tendency to talk too much. I don't want to overwhelm her even more than is already happening. She examines her room, taking everything in but not giving anything away. She sits herself in a little chair at the end of the bed and looks up and down the walls. I have no idea whether she likes what she sees or not. She is playing her cards rather close to her chest at the moment. Fair enough. That's her prerogative.

Helen leans across the bed and comments on the back garden, and I am struck again by what a weird position foster carers like me are in.

'That's a really good bit of garden you've got there. A real bit of wilderness. It must be great for the children. Plenty of space to play.'

It's meant as a compliment, I know, but somehow it feels intrusive and judgemental. 'A bit of wilderness' seems like a criticism of my gardening skills and lawn management rather than the reality of three – and often four children – and their friends and two dogs trampling across it the whole time. Actually, I'm very pleased with the way the garden is looking, borders neatly edged and containers in full bloom. Her comment jars a little, and I know that I am just feeling defensive. Mostly social workers behave impeccably, but sometimes their professional curiosity can come across as overstepping a boundary. I feel protective of my 'patch' all of a sudden. My home is my castle, after all. I would probably be the same inside someone else's home, but their eyes seem to dart everywhere, as though they are probing every nook and cranny. I once had one who went through our kitchen bin to see how well we did with the recycling. And I have watched another lean over to read the address on an envelope in the hallway.

But nothing so untoward happens here.

'Eden, this seems like a lovely room,' Terry says. Even though she is in the role of assistant, she is respectful and poised, and doesn't seem overly curious. I like the fact that she doesn't add, 'You're a lucky girl,' because there is nothing lucky about being born into a setting that results in you having to go into care because your basic needs are not being met or you have experienced abuse of some sort. I never need to hear gratitude from a foster child and it saddens me when I hear foster carers say that their foster children are not grateful; grateful for what? Why should they feel the need to display gratitude towards a responsible adult doing what they should?

Eden's expression is deadpan; nothing whatsoever seems to shift on her face. I wouldn't like to play her at poker. I notice that Daria, too, is saying very little. She also gently observes Eden whenever she can do so without being intrusive. It is interesting – and, to me, impressive – that she is holding back. I find it difficult to deal with any situation when the adults speak over and across a child about the child's life of being in care. Eden may not be giving much away, but I know she is taking it all in.

As we walk out of the room I notice Eden take another look backwards into it; she gives the coloured wardrobe a lingering glance, as though something is bothering her about it. If it were alive, and a person, she might not quite trust it. Her upper body seems to tense slightly as she looks, though it is a barely perceptible change. I only notice because I am watching her so carefully. She still says nothing, but I sense that she doesn't like it. She is evidently too polite or unsure of herself to draw attention to it. When our visitors have gone and the older children are back, I will get the boys to move it out. The last thing I want is for her to feel uncomfortable in 'her' space. Experience has taught me not to confront something like this straight away. It could be anything. When I was little I had to have the wardrobe door shut tight in order to go to sleep at night. I don't know what I thought might escape from inside it, but we all have these tiny anxieties. Part of my job is to minimise them for Eden where I can.

We walk into the bathroom, which is located right next door to Eden's room. I have old drawings, in frames, of naked women on the walls. They are from the 1930s and, in my view, a wonderful mix of ink and pencil life drawings. I love them. Helen and Terry look and say nothing, though I think I see the faintest of frowns cross Helen's brow, as though there is something inappropriate or distasteful about them.

Daria says, 'I like your pictures; they're beautiful.'

I really think I'm going to like working with Daria. She is a rule-breaker, I can tell. I get a little fed up with the rules around fostering, some of which make life a little unnatural in a household. We are not allowed to walk around in our underwear or a towel. From a safeguarding point of view, I get it. Of course I do. But from the practical perspective of living together in a house, it is less straightforward. When the children shower, they do sometimes bomb back to their rooms in a towel. I don't blame them. It is much easier to dress in the comfort and privacy of their own room than drag everything into the bathroom. To my mind, it is healthy for a child to see a human form – we all have them, after all. For me the pictures are important as well as being beautiful in themselves, and I am glad that Daria likes them too.

Eventually we head downstairs and sit back round the kitchen table. I encourage Eden and the dogs to go into the garden room once more. I make more coffee and sit down.

Daria smiles. 'Why are there two of you here?'

Nice and direct. I like that, too. I have been wondering the same thing, especially knowing how under-resourced children's social care is.

Helen smiles in return. 'My manager, knowing that this was a tricky one because Eden's mother is in prison, just wanted you to feel safe.'

I resist the temptation to laugh.

Daria creases her forehead. 'I don't think prisoners can come out when they feel like it. The last time I looked, anyway.'

Helen rolls her eyes in a gesture of submission and shared understanding of the ridiculousness of the situation. 'Yes, I know – but what can we do?'

'I thought it was a bit off, too,' Terry says. 'But I wasn't going to complain. I enjoy gleaning as much experience as I can outside, or I end up staying in the office – never meeting the children and foster carers.' She pauses for a moment before making her next, rather bold statement. 'And that, of course, is dangerous. The children are the reason we are here.'

I glance at Eden, who is bonding extremely well with Dotty and Douglas. The Jackahuahuas have clearly accepted her without question. I suspect they are going to be very important in the next few weeks.

I relax. I tingle with delight at being surrounded by these wonderful women who totally get it – who thoroughly understand the job we are all trying to do here under difficult circumstances. I am sorry for any of my earlier doubts, and remind myself that cynicism isn't a very becoming trait.

All is good in my little world – for now, at least.

Chapter 3

'We're back!'

As if I might not notice. The children arrive home in a mass of discarded school bags, coats and jettisoned shoes. The latter have been kicked roughly in the direction of the huge box in the hallway that is meant to contain them, but which they never quite make it into.

'Shoes,' I call out, though I know it will go unheeded. The box has become a semi-permanent home to two pairs of stinky trainers that the boys are not emotionally ready to throw away, but are now far too small to wear. The boys can grow a foot taller in a few months and have been known to skip a shoe-size in between purchases.

Jackson has recently done an about-turn, and changed his lifestyle quite dramatically in the last few weeks. After all my nagging at him to clean his teeth, he had to have a filling to believe me that it was important. Now he wears braces and keeps them impeccably clean, so much so that his orthodontist is genuinely impressed. Smelly trainers aside (and I feel sure that they will be gone soon), he is turning into a rather lovely young man.

Vincent, though, has hit what I and all my friends with sons call his 'gaming year'. He got a PlayStation for Christmas and, basically, we haven't seen him since. I hear him shouting and laughing, though his language is rather interesting: he seems fluent in dockyard. Occasionally I call up, 'Language, Vincent!'

A contrite, 'Sorry Mum,' floats back down the stairs, and then he carries on.

When Jackson went through *his* gaming year I was worried. I missed him, just as I miss Vincent now. They go, quite suddenly, from snuggling on the sofa to 'see ya'. Jackson's year in the digital wilderness has taught me not to worry so much. Gradually he began to come back down to see us more, then bit by bit he got a little bored – and I eventually realised that he gamed to chat to his friends. It's really hard pulling apart the general fears of technology. I worried that he would be ruined or abused online. I know he is fairly clued up and his school have been excellent at informing the children about the dangers lurking on the internet. Because I foster, I have attended training on 'online abuse' and they sometimes send out alerts if there is a new thing out that children should be kept away from. So I'm okay – but, like most parents, I know that there is plenty more I still need to know and learn.

I was reading the Children Act that came out in 1989. I know – I'm a riot at parties. But I find these documents interesting – especially as this was written before we had mobile phones and access to the internet. There is no clear guidance or policy on how to really keep our children and young people safe or what their rights are. It's a tricky path to find a way through to informing and trusting our young people, while keeping up with the speed of new threats to their safety via technology.

Thankfully, Lloyd is a graphic designer and is up to date with the latest technical developments – unlike me. Because of the nature of his job, our home is well resourced with Apple products and high-tech gadgets. But we are lucky; not everyone is in this position, and I often worry for the older foster carers who struggle to understand what's going on. The average age for a foster carer is 53 years for women and 54 years for men – yes, the *average* age, and, when I last looked, this isn't the savviest age for the latest digital trends. We could really do with some younger foster carers in the field, but I fear that, until they make it more financially viable, young people saving up for deposits for a house can't manage the financial commitment of looking after foster children and all that goes with it.

The children head directly to the kitchen; it's a foraging time of day. I'm in the garden room with Eden – they haven't seen us yet. Although I have told Eden all about the rest of the family, she is an only child, and these are the final moments before built-in siblings become a reality for her. I feel a little like David Attenborough, observing from a safe distance, as I note their antics. Lily starts an argument with Jackson about which of them is having the last cookie from yesterday. There are four in a pack, and until earlier today there were only three children to consume them – a fact well noted since Daniel's departure. Having a 'spare' available provides a neat opportunity for an argument. Even in good humour, their scratching at each other can become annoying. Jackson jumps up and sits on the kitchen surface by the plate rack, while Vincent drinks a huge glass of water, then goes to the bread bin to see if there is anything to put in the toaster, emerging with a couple of waffles. Jackson breaks the last cookie in half and offers one half to Lily. Rather than receiving the treat gratefully, Lily decides that she wants to measure it to make sure she doesn't have less; blimey, were we all this petty? I guess we must have been.

Jackson looks up and sees Eden and me. He nudges Lily and signals to Vincent, and slowly they gather themselves to peek round and take their first look. The tables are turned and they now become the observers for a moment. Eden is sitting on the floor with her back to them, and I am surprised to see that they all seem genuinely intimidated. A hush has descended. The squabbles are over now as they work out their next move.

When they were younger they would not bat an eyelid at saying hello and jumping straight in – no self-consciousness and no standing on ceremony; but now that they are at secondary school, they have developed a shyness and reserve.

Lily calls it 'social anxiety'. I wonder if naming every aspect of their development puts a strange spin on life. I daren't say that or she will jump down my throat. She is the most opinionated in the family (after me), a strident vegetarian and rainbow child. Her political awakening means that we find ourselves being corrected on terms we didn't know were correctable. I will say something that I don't realise is objectionable, and perhaps even felt was flattering. Something like, 'Hasn't Sophie got amazing hair?' only to be called out by Lily, who will take great delight in explaining, 'You're gender stereotyping and objectifying her.' How times have changed. I remember my adopted mum giving up on the generational transitions when I stopped wearing baggy granny knickers and started to wear midis. It's forever changing and, my word, the world is a complicated place to negotiate. What I wouldn't give to be having the same granny knickers midis debate now. And don't even get me started on thongs.

I smile at my three perhaps-not-quite-so-grown-up-after-all teenagers and wave reassuringly at them. Eden, who I swear has not altered her facial expression once all day long, turns around to see who is there. Carefully, and with an attempt at being gentle, the others come in. Fortunately, the dogs have no 'social anxieties' and can't wait to greet the children, which seems to amuse Eden, though her reactions are very difficult to judge. Doug is a kisser and we all try to stop him, but Jackson still can't resist going in for a smacker, finding it hilarious that Doug wants a snog. We all say 'Yuck,' and, 'Ew, don't let him do that!' but Jackson is lying on the floor with Douglas on his chest before we know it. I look at Eden and offer up a shrug and what I hope is a comical rolling of the eyes. She stares at me, but I am sure I detect a flicker of a shift. Maybe.

I stay for a few minutes more while the older children make themselves comfortable. Lily likes the swing seat; she will happily sit on it gently rocking for hours. It's a bit like trampolines: a rhythmic movement that can be quite soothing, especially to a child who has experienced trauma. Vincent sits sprawled across two beanbags and eats his waffles. I notice Eden watching them, her eyes resting first on one, then the next. This is good. I like my new arrivals to feel safe and reassured, of course, and sometimes watching how the older children live their lives here is better than me rambling on about 'how we do things in this house.' I worry that approach can be a bit overwhelming. I decided long ago not to do what a lot of fellow foster carers do and say, 'The rules are on the inside of the cupboard door or pinned to the fridge.'

When I was a child my adopted mother dropped me at my maternal grandparents' house once. I had never met them and, until I was standing outside their door, I didn't even know they existed. My adopted mum was going through some kind of psychosis at the time and had dropped my adopted sibling with his grandparents in Blackbird Leys in Oxford. I found myself further outside

Oxford, on a council estate, at a door with a note in my hand and a carrier bag. My grandparents were horrified. They whisked me round the back of the house through a gate and sat me in the garden with an orange squash while they called the Children's Department. I was taken straight into a foster placement: a busy house full to the brim with – in my young mind's memory – rude children. I was sat on a stool in the kitchen and given a clipboard with 'The Rules' on. A long list of things I could and couldn't do. It hadn't even occurred to anyone that I might not actually be able to read. I had missed so much school and, unknown to any of my educators at the time, I am dyslexic. I sat in silence in that horrible busy kitchen panicking about what the rules were. It has stayed with me as an experience that I wouldn't want to put anyone else through.

Consequently, we have very few rules. The ones we do have are more for safety, alongside the ones we signed up to agree to implementing when we did our 'Form F' and 'Panel for Approval', part of the preparation for being judged suitable as foster carers.

When I was teaching, I used to watch my colleagues announce their rules and expectations, or put them into their projects. To my students I would simply say, 'Do your best, and come and see me if you need support.' It amuses me when I sit in the reception waiting areas in secondary schools. I've sat with a wry smile as I read such inspirational mottoes as *A building with four walls and tomorrow inside* or *Sowing the leaders for tomorrow* or my personal favourite, *Nurturing an exciting future for the world*. I always wonder about the child who just wants to do okay – as I once did. Surely we need more of those than a world full of leaders? What a terrible place that would be.

After my experience of sitting on the stool with a clipboard I must have decided simply not to *do* rules, which may go some way towards explaining why I was known as a 'Wild Child' in my teens. So, I still avoid 'rules' as such, and avoid referring to anything directly as a 'rule'. I am much more inclined to say, 'We need to do this because...'

I busy myself retrieving their lunchboxes from the detritus in the hallway and stand at the sink washing them up. It gives me a chance to observe how the children begin to accommodate Eden. To my surprise, Vincent goes towards the cupboard where we keep the games and pulls out KerPlunk – where players take turns removing a single straw from the tube while trying to stop marbles from falling through into their tray. It's a game I remember playing in the 1970s but only at friends' houses; we never had such boxes of joy in our home. Does he know that you can't plug it in?

'Good idea, Vince.'

They all demonstrate enthusiasm at this suggestion, and set it up on the small IKEA coffee table. Very soon I hear laughter. Lots of it. Perfect, I think. Eden joins in with the game, taking her turn. I don't hear her voice, and I don't hear her laughter with the others, but I hope that maybe she's laughing on the inside. I tell myself that from her micro-movement body language she is enjoying being included, even if she doesn't speak. I hope she is also excited by the prospect of having three older children to be with. Between them they do the talking and the encouraging for Eden.

'Are you ready, Eden? It's your turn.'

'You've touched that straw, but are you sure it's the one you want to move?'

She doesn't answer, but moves are made, nevertheless. Vincent is the winner of the first game, but with Eden a close second.

'Again?' Lily suggests.

I get on and make tea, leaving them all to it. The children know that with a new arrival I would have checked ahead of them coming what they like to eat – and so far I haven't failed. This evening I have gone for the good old favourite: chicken nuggets, chips and beans. Eden doesn't eat her beans – but children can be sensitive to a brand-particular taste, and these are reduced salt. She has some food inside her, and that's good.

The evening pans out in a relaxed and easy way. Lloyd is away on a business trip until tomorrow evening and that gives me time to spend with Eden. Lloyd's work as a graphic designer takes him to different parts of Europe to help set up a number of trade shows. He is back and forth a great deal at the moment, mainly staying away in hotels. He tells me that it's not all glamour, and that travelling is jolly hard work, but the cities he is visiting sound exciting and far removed from the reality of caring for four children around the clock. Still, it is nice to have the bonding time.

Daria calls after dinner on my mobile. It's her own time and I appreciate her support; she just wants to know how it's going.

I don't ask Eden to have a bath or anything more than to relax on this first evening. That can wait. It's the teenagers who hum. Younger children are not generally smelly unless they have been totally neglected, and we have certainly looked after a few of those. One child smelt so badly in the groin area that I first had to go to the loo to be sick, then spend a great deal of time convincing and coaxing the child to have a bath, or even a little wash. It transpired that this child had been sexually abused and the abuse had always taken place in a bathroom, which understandably made bathrooms an undesirable place to be.

Though I have been critical of my fellow foster carer in the past, Janey has clearly done right by Eden – she is clean and in clean clothes, even if she has nothing additional with her. I keep a bag of spare clothes in the guest room, just for occasions like this. I know that there is a new pair of pyjamas in there that one of Lloyd's kind relatives bought Lily for Christmas without realising that Lily was too big for them. It was unlucky for Lily at the time, but fortuitous for Eden now. I take them out and put them on Eden's bed for later. I plan to take Eden shopping tomorrow and, if she seems okay, pop into one of the big department stores for a drink and cake. Why not?

After dinner the children do their homework and then quickly return to Eden for more games. Good on them. I am particularly impressed with Vincent's uncharacteristic restraint in tearing himself away from a virtual world to remain in this one for a while. So far at least, none of the children have commented on, or even acknowledged, Eden's lack of communication. Part of me thinks it's odd that they have said nothing, but maybe children just aren't as judgemental as adults. Maybe they don't see it as an issue and can happily communicate through play. It seems that way so far. Once the delights of KerPlunk have been exhausted, Eden sits in the sitting room by the footstool with a box of Lego, thoughtfully provided by Jackson. She isn't concentrating on the Lego, though: she is watching us.

I sit down with a cup of tea and try hard not to make that sound we women make when we reach a certain age – a sort of huffing sigh that never used to escape from my lips until recently. I am doing my best to hold at bay the ageing traps. I buy some of my clothes from New Look and mix them up with what might be considered more age-appropriate pieces in order to avoid becoming middle-aged in dress sense. What even is middle age?

I reach for the remote control. I have to confess I hardly watch the TV, but I know that on the whole, most children who come into care have watched a lot of TV. Some children I have looked after have had a meltdown if they miss the start of *EastEnders*, or 'Enders', as it is often called. I wonder if their parents grew-up watching Enders and they somehow think that life really is that chaotic and full of drama. These programmes make me feel giddy. I never watched them when I was young – I was too busy going out and having fun. For some children in care, screen time has meant YouTube rather than traditional TV. In any case, I try to find a programme that isn't full of scary drama. I think Eden's probably had enough of that in recent weeks. We watch a documentary programme about crabs in South America. Eden quietly sits and watches me, the television providing only a partial distraction.

Bedtime comes. The next tricky moment arrives. I reach out to hold her hand. She looks at it but does not take it. Does not react at all, in fact. Okay, I think. We need to build our trust and that is not going to happen overnight. The other children all say 'night'. It's very sweet. Vincent, who normally keeps his distance from new arrivals, makes a point of coming across to say goodnight to Eden. I watch her face colour a little as he beams at her.

'Hope you sleep well, Eden. We can do more playing tomorrow.'

I have no idea where this charm has come from, suddenly, but I love hearing him do this.

We walk upstairs – not holding hands, me leading. 'It's time to clean your teeth,' I say.

Eden ignores me and heads straight to the loo. When she's finished, she walks right past me and gets into her bed. She glances at the empty space where the wardrobe was and gives a little nod. Approval, perhaps. She pulls the duvet round her as tight as she can and faces away from me. It's the first night. It's not a battle we need to have – yet.

'I will leave the landing light on, and the door open.'

I hear not a peep from her after that. I quietly come back three times throughout the evening to check on her – the final time just before I go to sleep myself. She has not moved so much as an inch.

It's morning before I know it. I wonder how the night has been for Eden.

I run around waking the children up. There are the usual moans from Lily, and a more pleasant sound from the boys. Lily is not a morning person. I have simply learned to accept this, and stopped confronting her. She used to be very rude. Experience has taught me that she is much better if she is able to wake up at her own pace, uninterrupted; but of course, in actual life that can't always be the case. I do worry for her in later life, and hope we can get past these traces of her neglect so she can live a good life and hold down a job one day.

Vincent asks straightaway how Eden is. I walk towards her room to peep round the door and find her sitting on her bed, fully dressed, with her hands folded neatly across her lap. She has been entirely silent as she has got herself ready. Her eyes still bear the traces of redness that I noticed yesterday and I wonder if she has been crying overnight. I hope not. I certainly didn't hear anything. She's braving this out, though; there is evidently a toughness to her.

'Would you like to take Eden down to breakfast?' I ask Vincent.

He smiles and holds out his hand, as naturally as I do – and, to my shock, she takes it. Well played, my boy. Who knew Vincent would be the secret weapon? I watch the two of them, my long, gangly boy and this tiny little girl, walk down the hall together. It looks like the start of a beautiful film.

The others eventually come down, too, Jackson fully showered, dressed and smelling of Lynx Gold. I wonder how long it will be before he learns that less is more. Lily is still busy grumbling about something, I don't worry myself with what. In the mornings everything is everyone else's fault. I do my best to tune out from the general disgruntlement. *Patience, Louise*. My little internal mantras have already begun for the day.

Vincent shows Eden the choice of cereals. 'We have all these. You can choose whichever one you want.'

Eden takes a fraction of a second and then points at the Coco Pops. The sugariest and least breakfasty of the boxes on offer. Of course she does. No judgement necessary here, thank you. As a foster mum I have to work from a different place to most birth mums. I have to keep them eating and learn what they like as we go on, adapting frequently. Sugary breakfast is better than no breakfast. We can wean onto the healthier stuff later, when I have worked out her tastes. In this case, there wasn't a great deal of information in her file. Often what's written in the referral isn't accurate or is out of date anyway. I know that my own children are more than capable of suddenly announcing that they hate a particular food or meal that was perfectly acceptable a week ago. Even a favourite can suddenly lose status as flavour of the month, seemingly for no reason at all. Coco Pops it is.

I get a bowl from the cupboard and put it in front of her. Vincent, still being attentive, asks her what size spoon she would like, perhaps drawing on his own memory of his small cutlery set that is still in the drawer. She chooses the big spoon, but Vincent brings out his old Winnie the Pooh set – just in case. His judgement is proved right. She prefers it, and the size suits her little hands far better. He'll be up for a Nobel Prize, soon.

When the children have gone to school – Lily moaning all the way out the door over some perceived injustice – I clear up and explain to Eden that I have a few chores and a little bit of work to do, and then we will head into town to find her some new clothes. There is no change in her facial expression at all. That sure is one heck of a poker face.

In half an hour I manage to clear away breakfast, run around and grab all the washing, put a load on, make the beds and air the rooms. I leave Eden to do more exploring of the toys in the garden room, in the good company of Dotty and Doug. Just as I am on my way back down the stairs, my mobile goes. It's Daria.

'Good morning, Louise. How is she?'

I move out towards the garden, away from Eden, before I make my reply. I let Daria know how it all went.

'She's barely said a word since she arrived, but I think she enjoyed herself with the kids last night. Either she slept like a log – literally – or she didn't sleep at all. It's hard to know. She doesn't react to anything, so it's difficult to judge. But she does seem to have bonded with Vincent and held his hand this morning.'

'That's good. We all know that these things take time.'

Daria promises to keep checking in. I note that Helen, Eden's social worker, is yet to call, but Daria has phoned twice in less than 24 hours.

I return to the housework. I put some pencils and A4 printing paper on the kitchen table and say to Eden that I won't be long and that I would love it if she drew me a flower.

Once the last few bits are done, I zip upstairs and grab my bag, making sure my purse is in it. I've been caught out several times when I'm rushing only to get to a shop and realise that I have left my purse behind at home. With a new placement I always have what I like to think of as controlled excitement – or as Lily would have it, 'new placement anxiety'. Everything is about anxiety; maybe we have it more than we realise. Eden takes everything (and me) in her stride. She has done as asked and drawn a flower. It's quite an involved drawing for a five-year-old – more than a simple daisy shape. I can't determine exactly what kind of flower it is, but she's definitely put some time and effort into it.

'That's very pretty, Eden. I think we should put it up on the fridge.'

She seems pleased to have her work displayed in this way, holding her hands behind her back as if she is a learned connoisseur perusing the work of a grand master in an art gallery.

We head off into town. I park the car in the basement of the car park, heading straight down there first. I realised a long time ago that most human beings are actually sheep in disguise. We are a race of sheep-people who follow each other around. Most drivers follow the car in front of them, circling round and round the car park waiting for a space. Actually, the basement is usually free and I find myself heading down instead of up on entry. On this occasion I am proved right, and head straight into a space. I am victorious. Winning at life today. These things mean a lot to me. I wonder what Eden makes of my buoyant mood. We get the ticket together. Maybe, like so many of the children who have stayed with us over the years, she will get to the stage where I give her the change and she gets the ticket from the machine. I hope so. It's all part of growing up. Patterns repeat.

The fostering allowance really only allows for the cheaper end of the shopping options. When my sons were little I spent my hard-earned cash on clothes from John Lewis: good quality items that I managed to hand down from Jackson to Vincent and then on to friends. The clothes we buy from the large, cheaper shops have no substance to them, and I will be lucky if they last one season – but I try to avoid spending too much of my own money on foster children's clothing now. I used to do it because I felt sad that they didn't have nice quality items, but of course I never recouped the money. In fact, one social worker told me specifically to shop only at Primark or the Wednesday market. This 'advice' still annoys me. I know that we need to be careful consumers and pay the right price for a t-shirt that will last, but I don't want to feel that what I wanted for my own children I can't offer to the ones that are in my care. Instead of the smart department stores they get pop-up shops where clothes are slung on the floor, piles are knocked over and the fabric can sometimes feel offensively poor quality – but as always, what are foster carers meant to do? We are caught between a rock and a hard place. I do often pay out of my own money for their expensive trainers and so on – foster children need the labels as much as other children, perhaps more so. They need to belong, not to be continually reminded of their difference – already marked out emotionally, they don't need to be separated financially, too.

We walk around one of the lower-end clothing stores and I try very hard to ignore the provenance of the clothes, pushing the thought of children in a sweatshop away. I watch Eden pretend not to be interested – until we walk towards the accessories. Fluffy handbags and pencil cases, hairbands with daisies, brightly coloured beads and – wow, a whole pen set somehow made to look like different coloured fluffy unicorns. I hang around the area a bit, hoping that she takes the bait. Eden picks up the packet of pens and holds them towards me, and without looking at me manages to convince me she must have them. It's quite a feat of non-communication.

'Pop them in the basket, Eden. They look good, don't they?'

We walk to the nightclothes. I pick up a packet of three pyjamas with – guess what? – more fluffy unicorns adorning them. I grab some packets of knickers and socks and move towards the dressing gowns. Lily would have died inside if I had selected a pink one for her, the born feminist. It is a surprise to me that, after being drawn to the unicorns, Eden doesn't want pink. She looks at the pillar-box red fluffy dressing gown and I, of course, put it in the basket, before changing my mind and deciding in the interests of practicality to wrap it across my arm. Nothing else would actually fit into the basket otherwise. After a few essentials and a selection of leggings and tops, I will Eden to eye up the little dresses I have already spied. I had sons, so no scope for pretty dresses. My now grown-up stepdaughters didn't want pretty dresses; Lily hates them, and always has. I know this shopping trip is about Eden and not me – really, I do – but I cross my fingers and hope that she will want to wear a lovely dress and I can enjoy the experience vicariously. To my delight, she does. At last I have a dolly to dress up! No, Louise, that's terrible, my internal voice reminds me – she is her own person. But she will look so sweet in the little dresses.

After our shopping success I take her to what we are, in our family, inclined to call a 'costa-lotta' coffee shop for a drink and cake. It is a ritual that is standard Allen practice – but also something I like to do with a new arrival early on as a treat. I describe the concepts of a fruit smoothie and a milkshake, in complicated and expressive explanations that are probably hilarious for anyone else watching (but are accompanied by no feedback whatsoever from their intended audience, which I am already getting used to). Eden chooses the banana shake, and, after ages staring at the rather mean cake selection, she offers a slight, almost imperceptible nod towards the cherry chocolate slice. I can no longer eat such richness in the morning and would like to see some reduction in my waistline before I get too old to wear some of my gorgeous clothes, so I forego one myself, though she has definitely made the right selection. We sit down at a little table and I can sense that Eden is enjoying the experience, though she continues to say nothing. I think it's important that children experience many social settings. Has she been out to cafes and restaurants much before? I have no real way of knowing, but she certainly seems at ease in here and isn't overwhelmed by the occasion. She carefully eats her cake. I notice that she is sitting bolt upright. This makes me smile.

She didn't do this at home and I hope that meant she felt comfortable there – and that she cares enough when she's out to make an effort. I already find this little girl fascinating.

We arrive home in time for lunch. Once the very excited dogs have calmed down and been out for an obligatory wee, I hold up several options of cheese, ham or peanut butter, to place in Eden's sandwich. She doesn't look up, but when I put the selection back on the butcher's block she shoves the peanut butter jar back with a loose fist of fingers. Okay, understood. I feel a little bit like Elliott interacting with ET in the beginning, when the little alien first arrives from space and hasn't yet learned to speak. I get the bread out and begin making the sandwiches. I can't resist playing around with food presentation, especially with little children. Crustless half-triangles offer a nice little bite without having to nibble round the chunky crusts. Eden plays her part and eats everything up. I am grateful for these small victories. If I am feeding her, that is a good start.

Once lunch is cleared I get the craft box out of the cupboard in the garden room. I sit down next to where Eden is and begin explaining what we have to work with, then give her the choice of sewing or painting. Without any warning, she puts her little hand on my wrist and settles it for a few seconds. Then it's gone. I have a little lump in my throat and fight off the leaking tears. She is a sweetheart. I pull out the wooden pegs and scraps of coloured felt that she has indicated with a flick of the hand, and we begin making peg dolls.

She uses felt-tip to make a face, and then watches me as I cut out a long skirt for my peg doll. She is very keen to make hers for herself, before creating another. Soon we have a peg doll family. Isn't it funny how we are all programmed to create what we think a typical family looks like? I had the impression that she had lived just with her mum, but there seems to be a dad figure in there, too. We while away a happy hour creating the figurines, finishing them off with glued buttons and ribbons.

I make a snack of grapes and Ritz biscuits. She likes that combination and quickly bolts it down. Entirely different behaviour from when she was out, but lovely to see, none-theless. My mobile begins to ring, so I tell her that she can get down from the kitchen table. She does so dutifully, selects a picture book from the shelf, and heads to the garden room, where she arranges herself on a bean bag. The dogs can't resist a lap opportunity, so Douglas jumps up next to her and waits for her to somehow give him permission to sit on her tiny lap. She sits with the book open, cuddling Douglas. I love dogs. He is sitting with his head across her arm, and Dotty is at her feet. It makes a nice picture. My call is over in a minute – a quick work question that is easily resolved – and so I move around the kitchen, tidying up. It gives me a few moments to decide what to make for dinner this evening. I look at the Caribbean seasoning, then the Levi Roots cookbook. A quiet little sound interrupts my planning. I listen harder: it's Eden, talking to somebody. Douglas, perhaps. They were very cosy a few moments ago. But I look down and Douglas is there at my feet. Is she talking to herself, then?

I crane my neck to see around the door without disturbing her. She is crouched down next to the 1930s fairground duck that stands forgotten in a corner of the garden room, a lump of metal that used to terrify the other children when they were younger. I found the duck years ago in a junk shop in Portsmouth. I often went into the shop to gaze at interesting items, and one day this monstrosity of a duck caught my eye. I had Jackson with me, still small enough to be strapped into a buggy. To this day I have no idea what compelled me to buy the thing, but make the purchase I did, and the shopkeeper helped me to wedge it safely into the pushchair. It was heavy and awkwardly shaped, and I remember it being quite an ordeal to get it home. Back at home, I washed it and put it in the corner of the stairs, where I thought it looked quite fetching. Jackson did not agree. He burst into tears and refused to go up the stairs at all until it was removed. I have not met a child until Eden came along who wanted to make friends with the duck – but that's what it looks like she is trying to do. In fact, she is telling him earnestly that her mum is called Ashley and she's gone away.

'She's going to be away for a while, so I am staying here with you for now.'

They are the first real words that she has spoken.

Chapter 4

It is early morning on day four of Eden's time in the Allen household, and so far so good.

Vincent is already up and about. He's at an age where I can control his device usage in the evenings and ensure that he still goes to bed early enough to get a full night's sleep (unlike his siblings). He is a delight in the morning.

'Hi mum, you okay?'

Oh, I adore that boy and I will enjoy every second of him until he undergoes the metamorphosis that will transform him into the teenage boy that I know he has to become soon. He helps me by getting the breakfast things out while I see to the dogs. When it is time to wake Jackson, I have to knock on his door three times, yelling like a banshee to have any hope of getting a reaction.

Knock, knock. 'Jackson, SCHOOL.'

The final time I knock, pause, and then go in. I don't want to wake up Eden just yet. She is still settling and sleeping is part of that process. I'm also not entirely convinced that she *is* sleeping a great deal during the night. I think she pretends to be asleep when I do my rounds. Usually with a cat or two in tow, I tiptoe into each child's room last thing to check on them. I have had an inclination that Eden was awake, but with her eyes closed. There has been a certain stiffness to her sleeping position. A younger child might echo their baby sleep and stretch out with arms above their head. They can look a bit like a starfish. Not this little one. Rigid and tiny, with her duvet right up to her eyebrows, it's as if she is hiding, protecting herself. Perhaps she doesn't fall asleep until the small hours. It can't be easy in a new place, with all the mental burden she must be carrying. I'm glad she was able to 'chat' with Hueydewcy yesterday.

Finally, Jackson is up. He makes his procession to the bathroom. I run out quickly and warn, 'Don't be too long in the shower.'

He makes a gruff, more or less incomprehensible sound and proceeds to ignore me. Since he became a full-on teenager, his use of language seems to have regressed to a much more Neanderthal branch of communication. As I wait for him to come out of the shower, which takes just as long as it takes, in spite of me knocking on the door with helpful advice like 'A shower is meant to be quick, not like a bath,' or a more urgent, 'Jackson, I need to get in there,' he continues to not respond, other than to put Stormzy on really loud.

I head down the corridor, catching sight of myself in the mirror. I am sporting Indian cotton pyjamas with a batik leaf print, and carrying it off rather well, if I do say so myself. I love them because they are loose and not too hot. I am waiting for that 'particular' stage of my life to shower over me. I heard a woman on *Woman's Hour* tell Jane Garvey in graphic detail about her hot flushes – how her bed was soaked every night. Wow, that's something to look forward to. I also recall when I was a younger woman working at the university and older women 'of a certain age' could be quite difficult to work with. Male colleagues were cruel and ready to mock them because they were hot, red-faced and quick-tempered. I realised then what a difficult place the workplace is for women. At least, working from home and fostering, I'm not dealing with that level of misogyny and discrimination. Mind you, the women in question were horrible before they reached that stage.

Maybe my menopause will be like my early teen years. I grew up being told I was ugly, no one would want me, I had oily Jewish skin (Moroccan actually), and was fat. This last one was applied to me, even though clinically I was malnourished. I made a decision very early – when I was old enough to walk into town on my own – that I was going to smile. Just that. Not too much that I looked mad, but enough to make me look warm and friendly. I believed that if I worked hard on smiling, my face would change and I would be less ugly, and eventually I would look alright. I'm the same with the menopause. I keep telling myself that when it comes I am ready to embrace it. I am just going to keep smiling my way through it. Perhaps I still have a few years to go. Maybe it's not knocking at my womanhood's front door just yet. But being a hormonal woman in a house full of teenagers and challenging foster children is a great test for any woman's resilience, whatever stage of life they are at.

I finish contemplating my life and pyjamas, and knock and open Lily's door.

'Morning Lily,' I call out, in my usual, happy sing-song voice, my first line of defence in successfully managing the start to her day. If we get this part of the morning wrong, the whole day can go awry. Lily still needs so much support. Her early life of neglect has left her feeling a lot of shame and, of course, that can turn quickly into defensive anger.

When she was a small child she didn't have the routine of morning time or bedtimes. I removed the curtains when she first arrived in order to help align her body clock to the world order of day and night. I deliberately didn't tell the social workers until after my experiment, in case they took a dim view of my methods. I have been on the wrong end of people's apparently 'professional' opinions in the past. The conversations I have had about bedside lights, or if a foster child is allowed to sleep in a double bed, the many hours I have had to dedicate to a particular idea a social worker has had about attachment theory – oh, it goes on and on. My particular favourite is in cases of neglect. After a child has arrived and I have managed to persuade them to put clean clothes on, I must put the extremely soiled underwear and clothes *unwashed* in a plastic bag and give the artefacts back to the birth parent. Apparently that's the law, because technically they are the property of the birth parents. Yes, I know. It doesn't bear thinking about. I did – and still do – burn them when this happens. I don't want to pollute my washing machine or insult the birth parent. And, let's not forget, they have had their child removed. Can you imagine being presented with soiled items of clothing after your child has been taken away? Even if that parent wasn't able, for whatever reason, to meet the child's most basic needs, I always think that somehow the parent has been let down by our world, too, and doesn't deserve the 'gift' of a bag of festering fabric. So, for experiments that are not going to hurt anyone, I tend to just get on with it and send feedback if they have worked – which it did in Lily's case with the curtains. Eventually Lily's body clock began to link with the sun and moon, but I don't think she will ever deal with the days starting as most people do. I keep on trying, though; one day she will have to survive for herself out there, and no one will keep her on in employment if she's continually late or grumpy.

I exit Lily's room and determinedly suppress a silent yawn. I'm tired – there is always something about the emotional load of having a new child in the house to care for – but I don't want the children to *think* I'm tired, because then they are utterly ruthless. They can scent blood. If they sense I'm out of sorts then there is a co-ordinated, collective move to play up and send me into a spin.

Eden suddenly appears and yanks at my sleeve. She pulls me to the top of the stairs. She wants to get the dogs; I know that, but pretend that I don't – so that maybe if I keep guessing what she wants she will just come out and say it.

She doesn't.

I give in and open the sitting room door where the dogs sleep in their cosy little crate. If there was a canine version of *Elle Decoration*, this would make the centre spread. My friend has a sheepdog, a working dog who sleeps on newspaper in the cage. This is nothing like that. Oh no. My little four-legged friends have lined curtains around their bed, two coordinating pillows, and their own soft toys and teddy. The setup is quite a thing to behold. When I open the door there is always a pungent waft of sweaty dog waiting, so I dash to open the window before I let them out.

Eden can't wait for me to pull back the lock on the crate's door. She almost climbs into their bed in her eagerness to be reunited with Dotty and Douglas. The relationship between animals and traumatised children is stunning; it never fails to move me. I leave her to the dogs, then notice that Mabel, our cat, is stretching out on the sofa. She has very few feline characteristics – none of the superciliousness that our other cats have displayed. She hates going out at night, and she's actually quite affectionate. But she is also scared of everything that moves – and I'm fairly sure she believes she's one of the dogs. In actual fact she's a bit bigger than Douglas and Dotty, but they make a fine trio, nevertheless. I walk out into the hall towards the kitchen now with cat, dogs, and a little bright-eyed Eden in tow. I feel a little like the Pied Piper of Hamelin. I fling open the back door and tell them all to go and have a wee.

Eden looks at me, almost in the eye.

'Not you, you can use the loo,' I laugh.

The corners of her mouth turn upwards ever so slightly. You'd be hard pressed to call it a smile and it's the faintest of movements, but she has 'got' and enjoyed the joke, I'm sure.

Within a few minutes the house is full of activity. I still need to get Jackson out of the bathroom. I take the precaution of warning Eden that I'm going to shout up to Jackson – and that my voice will be very loud. She puts her hands on her ears in preparation, and now I do see a small smile. Still very 'linear' to anyone who isn't watching closely, but a smile nonetheless, I am sure of it.

'JACKSON!'

'WOT?'

I love him dearly – but seriously, what else does he think I'm calling up to him for? 'Are you OUT of the BATHROOM?'

He doesn't deign to reply, but I hear a slam of the bathroom door, which means it's free – success. There is a price to pay. I know that there will be clothes and towels everywhere. I look at Eden and roll my eyes. 'Men!' I say, sharing a conspiratorial moment with her. She almost smiles for a third time. I know I shouldn't be sharing my gender stereotypes in this way – and certainly not encouraging them to be complicit. But with the girls I take delight in letting them know about equality and that girls and women are *the ones*, ha. I think she instantly knows what I mean – and gives me a startlingly knowing look. For a moment I have the strangest sensation, as if we had been discussing this down the pub as equals. I am realising that trapped inside this quiet little girl is a big personality. Good. All the better for Eden.

I get the cereals out and set her up at the table. Vincent has the most incredible knack of arriving at the table just at the right time, exactly as food is being delivered. He appears almost simultaneously with the touch of the cereal packet on wood. I watch the two of them side by side for a moment. Eden evidently likes Vincent, and to his credit he is playing the big brother role brilliantly.

I have no idea what the men in Eden's life so far have been like – there is no mention of a partner for Ashley on file – but I often think that if a child has had the misfortune of a dominant, controlling – maybe violent – man in their life, then a Jackson or a Vincent is just what they need to help them understand that not all men are made the same way. I have worked continuously with my sons to make sure they have plenty of feminist credentials. Both cook and clean, and take responsibility for doing various domestic chores – though there is still plenty of work to be done. I hope that they are children who understand and acknowledge the burden that women bear in managing both home life and careers, in a way that many men still don't.

Vincent once designed a t-shirt for a school project with the words *I Respect Women* across the front. I was thrilled with the design and the sentiment, and felt really proud of him. Needless to say, it didn't necessarily sit comfortably with some of the slogans of his male peers. He ended up not submitting it to be manufactured. I think he lost his nerve in the end. I recognised his endeavour and can also acknowledge how difficult it would have been for a young lad to follow that through among his peers. I'm still proud of my boy and his capacity to be both ally and role model, though – then and now.

There is a little thud, thud on the wooden staircase leading to the kitchen. The steps are sluggish, reluctant. Lily is heaving herself into the day. She is really getting her teenager's wings, and presents a face like a wet bank holiday weekend. Say nothing, I counsel myself, knowing that this is the only way to get her through the next, crucial half hour or so. Anything critical coming from my lips could prove fatal.

Eden switches her gaze from Vincent, to Lily, then Douglas. She is drinking it all in, working out what's what, learning the rhythms of our household.

After they have finished I encourage them all to put their bowls and cutlery on the side near the dishwasher. One day I hope that, with a little encouragement, they, and Lloyd, may progress to the next step: understanding that the dishwasher door does, in fact, open and that they can actually put the dirty dishes in there by themselves. I look forward to that miraculous day. As I say, still work to be done on the chores front.

The fug of Lynx, recalling 'teenage boy' as much as African savannah, begins to disperse soon after the children depart for school. So, what's in store for Eden and me at home? I have a little work to do. How good is Eden going to be at occupying herself?

'Would you like to go and play in the garden room for a bit?'

At my suggestion she gets up and heads there. I leave her to it while I pick up messages and answer a few emails.

Daria has already left a message. *Hi Louise, how are you? Just seeing how you are getting on and if you need anything from me.* I think I might love Daria; she is so on it. Her consideration is reassuring. I wonder where Helen is – or Terry, she was nice. This is the start of day three for Eden in the Allen household and Helen still hasn't called. Hey ho. No harm done – all is currently well as far as I can see. I call Daria back. She answers immediately. She's in her car on speaker phone but is very happy to talk to me. She is always so happy and light, full of positivity. I wish all social workers came like this.

I update her with how Eden has continued to settle in well, but express my concerns about the fact that she won't talk.

'To the best of my knowledge she hasn't said a word to anyone human in the household, so apart from whispering to the dogs, and the odd word to a toy, she's not speaking.'

'She seemed very shy and it's still early days.'

'It is, but it's unusual not to have said a single word. So I've made an appointment for Eden at my GP's surgery this morning. She's going to have a bit of a check-up, and I want to make sure she hasn't got hearing loss problems – or maybe just wax in her ears. We've had a few children in the past who just need the wax out. But because I've heard her talking to Douglas and Dotty, I don't really think that's it – but I just want to rule it out – or make sure.'

'Yes. Good idea.'

'I need to try and understand why she doesn't talk. Something's going on there.'

'It may be wax in her ears; it may be an emotional reaction,' Daria says. 'It could settle down in a few more days as she relaxes and gets to know you all.'

I know that, and agree with her. So I won't be too hasty to jump to conclusions. Daria is such a sensible person – a mum as well as a professional social worker – who understands that sometimes issues with children are not always directly related to attachment. I think sometimes we can hang a label round a child's neck very quickly. Perhaps one that may be incorrect or demeaning – but, as so often in this sector, one that is sometimes necessary as the only way to get support and funding. A good label can often be the key to getting therapeutic support.

One little boy I knew was rejected by his adopters because they thought he had mental health issues. He was four and had been with his adopted family for a year. The adopters were frustrated with him not wanting to be cuddled, and his habit of rocking back and forth. They were driven to distraction by his crying, and the adoptive mum claimed to be scared of him. The adoptive parents personally funded a private child psychologist to do a review of his mental health, the outcome of which was essentially, *this child will never attach.* Never? As in never-ever? What a life sentence that could have been. With a prognosis like that, the placement disintegrated rapidly and the little boy was soon being collected from the end of the drive by his social worker.

He was placed with Betsy – a lovely Irish woman I know – whose husband had died a few years before, but she didn't stop fostering despite being on her own. She is my favourite kind of foster carer: warm, pragmatic and kind. After one evening with the little boy she realised the problem straight away and took him to the dentist, who immediately referred him to the hospital to have his baby teeth removed. They were so rotten. He had eight abscesses that were evidently causing him a lot of pain, as well as causing him to run a high temperature. I think of that story often, and I have become mindful always that we need to look at practical, physical things just as much as demanding 'therapy' when facing each obstacle.

I change the subject. 'Do you happen to know what's happened to Helen? I am surprised not to have heard from her.'

Daria explains that Helen works in a different office and offers to try and find out. The sooner the better, as far as I am concerned. It is a requirement that Helen completes a statutory visit while Eden is still new in her placement. Daria is sympathetic and supportive and promises to do what she can. I tend to pace around when I am on the phone, finding the rhythm of walking helps my clarity of thought, but as I move about with my phone pinned to the side of my head, I hear something: a voice, a little girl's voice.

'Hang on a sec, Daria.' I put my head round the garden room door an inch. Eden can't see me, as she has her back to the door. Hueydeweylouie is now wearing a bright blue duffle coat that was hanging over a chair, so that he looks like a kind of deformed Paddington Bear – and Eden is talking directly to him in earnest conversation.

I bolt back into the kitchen and whisper into the mobile, 'Eden is talking to Hueydewey again.'

'Hueydewey?'

'Hueydeweylouie actually, but Hueydewey for short. He's three feet high and made entirely of metal. Long story. Gotta go. I'll call you straight back.'

'Wow, okay. Let me know.'

I put the phone on the table and tiptoe back into position by the door.

'Baz was a bad man, Duck,' Eden explains, with an emphasis on 'bad' combined with a world-weariness better suited to an ageing country-and-western singer than a little five-year-old girl.

Right. I certainly need to know who this Baz is, then, I think, and how he fits into Eden's story. I need the rest of the paperwork from Helen because that name hasn't appeared anywhere as yet. I thought that Ashley was a single mum. There was no mention of a partner. Where's bloody Helen? I keep listening.

Eden goes on to tell the duck about her old room in her old house.

'Do you like where you sleep, Duck? My old room was very, very small. It was so small that it was only big enough to fit my mattress in with a few toys and no room to walk around. It was very, very dark in there. No windows. It's nice in here with lots of windows.'

A dull light bulb flicks on somewhere in my brain as I listen to her monologue, but I can't quite make the connection right now. A very dark room. A small space. It will come to me. At least I know for sure now that she does have a voice, but the only clue I really have is the name 'Baz'.

I send a quick text to Daria: *Is or was there somebody called 'Baz' in Eden's life? She is mentioning that name.* I haven't got time to chat properly now; I need to get Eden to the doctor.

Daria messages straight back that she will try and dig out more information to find out where Baz fits in to Ashley's setup. I sing-song into the garden room to make sure that Eden isn't disturbed unexpectedly.

'I see you've taken a shine to Hueydewey there. Would you like to have him in your room?'

Her eyes light up. Good. That will fill the space in the corner where the wardrobe was, and if it makes her feel better then I don't want to get in her way. It's a frightful thing, nearly the same size as her, and carnivalesque – but if she likes it, she likes it.

'Okay, we'll move him up there later. Before that, would you like to take the dogs for a little walk?' I say.

The tiniest of nods, but her eyes are still smiling.

'And then we will go to the doctors'. There may be a little wait in there, but there is a nice waiting room. He – or she –' (we never quite know which doctor we will see at the surgery these days), 'may want to check in your ears. Will that be ok?' I am very used to explaining everything to my children, in as much detail as I can. Sometimes I think they must assume I'm a bit over the top with the explanation of minutiae, but I want them to know exactly what we are doing and why at all times. How will they get to find out otherwise? Eden still doesn't know me, really, or how I roll. I know better than anyone that I can come across as a bit bonkers sometimes. But I'm an ex-care-child myself, and I still have those tendencies towards impulsiveness that are so much a part of the heightened vigilance experience. As a child I was always waiting to see who was coming into my room and, even now, if I hear footsteps heading towards my studio, a little patter against a tiled floor, I can easily slip straight back into my inner scared child. I know only too well how not having to deal with any 'surprises' can be a great relief for a child – hence my tendency towards over-planning, and over-explaining that planning.

Outside, Eden is determined to hold Douglas's lead and, since he is loving all this attention, Douglas is only too happy to oblige. Dotty is not so impressed with the arrangements, as she has to make do with me. Eden walks just a little bit behind me, now whispering to Douglas. I hear the name 'Baz' again. Sounds like he's got a lot to answer for, this Baz, whoever he might be. I listen a bit harder. I catch the odd word, 'horrible', 'hurt', 'people'. Hmm. My radar is on red alert. Then, 'lucky, lucky, lucky'. Does she mean that she is lucky now? I will have to think about this and tell Daria. Like a detective on one of those Sunday evening shows, I intend to get to the bottom of this.

We walk round the park slowly, me pointing out anything I can see which might be of interest to Eden. She takes it all in, but never responds. I spy one of the gardeners who helped control my trees when we moved in. I smile and give him a cheery wave, but Eden jumps and gets as close in to me as she can without actually touching me, almost cowering behind me. Though she took Vincent's hand to come down to breakfast, and she has tugged at my sleeve in the house to indicate direction, she is definitely reluctant to instigate physical contact. That's not unexpected in itself, but I am getting the feeling that something has happened to this little girl – something bigger than her mother being sent to prison – and we need to know what it is so that we can help.

Poor old Jim, who has done nothing wrong whatsoever, looks a bit concerned as Eden hides behind me. Jim isn't actually 'old' at all. In fact he seems like a rather lovely young man to me – fit and muscular from the physical gardening work, and maybe in his early twenties, perhaps about the same age as my son-in-law. He sports a beard and piercings alongside a few tattoos – you know the look. Nothing about Jim is remotely scary as far as I am concerned; he was very kind when he was working at the house. But Eden certainly doesn't like the look of him. Jim knows that I foster children and that some of them arrive with interesting behaviours, so I hope he will understand that this is not personal. I think almost everyone round here knows we have foster children; I'm never sure if that's a good or bad thing. I smile at Jim reassuringly, trying to indicate that he shouldn't worry about Eden's reaction – not so easy without being able to say anything directly, but I hope that he gets the message. Something about his appearance is intimidating Eden, though. Perhaps he resembles this Baz in some way. I am putting two and two together to make five, but I don't have much to go on at the moment.

When we get home I shut the dogs up and get myself and Eden to the car, ready to make our trip to the GP surgery. I put her on her booster seat and strap her in. We recently received an electronic memo from the Local Authority updating us on car safety laws, and I am mindful that I do it all properly.

In the doctors' waiting room there is another man with a beard. In fairness, just about every man of a certain age around here has a beard these days, so it isn't terribly surprising. But Eden certainly isn't comfortable about being near him, edging away to sit on the other side of me from where she first positioned herself. I watch her peer around me a couple of times – as if to check on him. Interesting.

The doctor – thankfully it is our usual one – is his usual lovely self. He sighs as he welcomes me into his consulting room and offers me a seat.

'Another one, Louise?'

I smile and explain my hypothesis for both audiences – Eden and the doctor – that Eden is newly arrived with us and she hasn't spoken very much yet, so we just wanted to check that there is nothing wrong with her hearing, or any other physical explanation. Behind Eden, I then explain in a sort of mouthing fashion, but not quite saying the words out loud, 'She has spoken to a toy.'

He nods. Message understood. He's used to my foibles by now. He checks her over. 'You seem chipper and in good health, young lady.'

Eden offers a shy smile in return.

To me he says, 'Her ears could do with some drops to loosen the wax, but no real concerns.' He suggests to Eden that she might like to play with the toys in the other room where the ladies in reception can see her, 'while I write out your prescription for a few ear drops.'

Eden dutifully obliges.

He closes the door gently behind her and asks me questions. I need little encouragement to open up and quickly explain that I am trying to get to the bottom of this Baz thing. We throw a few ideas around. He suggests 'Selective Mutism' as a possibility, a condition that I am not really familiar with.

'Does she have any marks anywhere on her body?'

It's something that years of experience have taught me to be on the lookout for, so I can answer him truthfully. I looked very carefully when she took a bath last night. 'She does have some red marks on her limbs, but they are very faint and I'm not worried.'

'Nothing you need me to have a look at, then.'

'I don't think so, no.' Next I offer my hastily thrown-together theories about bearded men.

'But no discernible reaction to adult men without beards?' he interrupts.

'Good question. And I'm not sure, to tell you the truth. She hasn't actually met Lloyd yet. He'll be home tonight. He's been away on business for a few days and I don't know that she's seen any others – apart from you. But she didn't react negatively towards you,' I say, looking pointedly at the doctor's clean-shaven visage.

'True,' he concedes.

'It's a good job Lloyd hasn't got a beard, I suppose,' I joke. 'No chance of him growing one, though: I was terrified of them as a child. I wouldn't go and see Father Christmas.'

'Yes, it's not that unusual – and maybe something as simple as that in young Eden's case. Let's hope so. Meanwhile, I'll make a referral to the paediatrics team at the hospital.' He breaks off from tapping into his computer to look up and smile. 'Which we both know may take a little while to come through.'

Over the next few days I watch Eden carefully whenever we are out and about. As we walk round the park or head into town I take note of the way she reacts to different people.

Two young women walk by us, in trendy tight ripped jeans and cropped T-shirts that show off tightly toned bellies. Like Jim, they sport tattoos. Both women have bleach-blonde hair, so bleached that it is almost white. One wears hers down and long; the other has hers tied up in a doughnut on top of her head. Eden looks suspiciously at these women, eyeing them up and down carefully while moving towards me – still not ready for a touch just yet. Perhaps they remind her of someone, or something, from her past. I put out my hand to touch her arm and test the water; she quickly moves away.

Back at home, after greeting the dogs, she heads to the garden room and begins to set up a tea party with Hueydewey.

She definitely likes that duck. A success, of sorts, I suppose. I watch for another few seconds as, even though it is made of unyielding metal, she tries to hug it. It's as big as she is, but she evidently doesn't seem bothered by its size. I resolve to move it to her bedroom for her, as promised.

Hearing, the sound of Lloyd's car, I tiptoe away once more. He is arriving back from his business trip, no doubt a little travel-weary.

'How was it?' I ask, greeting him at the front door.

'Well, the traffic was awful, especially coming through Hampshire.'

I make a sympathetic face. 'Can I get you something to eat?' I ask.

'Maybe later.' I know that actually means. He's had a cheeky McDonald's on the way back: his guilty pleasure. Well, we sat around in a coffee shop; I can't be too critical.

'Come and meet Eden – if I can drag her away from her new friend, that is.'

Lloyd raises a questioning eyebrow. 'Oh? One of the dogs?'

'She's getting on fine with the dogs, but no – of all things it's Hueydeweylouie, you know – that giant duck!'

But the frank conversation with Hueydewey the duck is evidently over, and Eden has now turned her attention to a doll from the toy box. She has it wrapped tightly in a doll's blanket, cuddling it as if it is a precious baby. I am sure now that this child has been well-loved; you can tell by the way children act out 'care' and 'nurture' with toys. She knows how to be kind, and she seems concerned that the little doll is comfortable and safe. It's very sweet.

Lloyd steps through behind me. I have, of course, forewarned Eden that he will be arriving this afternoon. Thankfully Lloyd has rearranged his 'I've been driving' face – that can look a little frightening if you don't know him.

He beams at her. 'Hello there, Eden. It's lovely to meet you at last.'

She glances up and gives a sort of smile in return. Not really intimidated at all. So it's not men in general, then. Just beards, or tattoos, or perhaps both in combination.

'Right. Let's get Hueydewey upstairs, shall we?'

Eden nods with enthusiasm.

As I go to move three feet of duck to its new position in Eden's bedroom, I notice that the metal is all wet. I pull my hand back and look up, wondering if we have a leak in the garden room – that would be a disaster. But I can't see anything dripping from anywhere above. I remind myself that it has been a lovely day and we haven't had any rain, and anyway, nothing else around the duck is wet. Perhaps something has been spilled, then. I reach for a tea towel, wipe Hueydewey down, and promptly forget about it. It is a 'nothing' incident within a long and busy day. There is certainly nothing that seems sinister or untoward about it.

The significance only becomes clear much, much later on.

Chapter 5

A couple of days later when Eden has been with us for just over a week, the others are still at school, and Eden and I are at home together. I have convinced my publisher that I really am busy working hard on the book, although I am in fact sitting with Eden at the kitchen table to do some art. Lloyd is away again, though not on business this time. He is also coping with long drives to the south coast to visit his ailing mother, who has recently had a hip operation. Given her age, recovery is slow. What doesn't help is that she lives in a three-storey house and is unable to climb the stairs at the moment. When Lloyd is there, he and a younger brother are spending time rearranging the entire house to adapt it to her new needs. He left early this morning. We are at a stage in life where between us we seem to be spending plenty of time caring at each end of the spectrum: both for our children and our parents.

Eden has been immaculately behaved in the short time she has been with us. 'Good as gold' is the way you might describe her: quiet, dutiful, happy to play with the others or occupy herself alongside Hueydewey – who is, at Eden's silent insistence, now standing on a chair so that he is on the same level as us up at the table, as if to join in with the art session. He's quite awkward to move around (Hueydewey has very definitely become a 'he' rather than an 'it' since Eden's arrival), but the palaver of dragging him from place to place around the house is outweighed by the comfort and enjoyment that Eden seems to get from 'his' presence. I also feel that she and I are starting to become good friends, though it all happens with very limited verbal communication on her part.

We have paper and pens spread out on the table, and Radio 4 is providing the entertainment, with voices from the afternoon play drifting across the room. It is a lovely time: very peaceful when the otherwise busy house is empty of all other humans. I have a cup of tea on the go. Eden has some well-diluted squash and a little bowl of grapes next to her. I am painting an idyllic picture, here, I know. Generally grapes are harder work to organise than crisps, but Eden is still behaving as a polite house guest and eating whatever is in front of her rather than expressing her own preferences. So, while I'm still making the decisions, grapes it is.

I am only half following the narrative of the play, which is about two detectives, an older one and his young rookie, who keep each other in check. I shift in and out of the plot. They are trying to resolve turf wars on an inner-city housing estate and have arrived at the scene to solve the crime of a dead dog. Any hurt to animals draws me in immediately, and I drift away from what Eden is doing for a moment to listen more closely to this part of the play. A short amount of time passes before she wafts the pieces of paper past my face as if to make a breeze, and as a way of getting my attention without calling my name or speaking.

I snap away from the fictional narrative and back into the here and now. I apologise for my temporary absence with a smile. 'Sorry, Eden. I got all carried away with the story for a moment there. Now, what have you been up to? What have we got here?'

She lays out three pieces of A4 paper on the table with a careful, deliberate placement, seeking my approval – or acknowledgement. Each one has a male form – or at least one that it is depicted wearing trousers. There are similarities between them in the colours she has chosen and the way she has drawn the hair. It is the same man.

My heart sinks and I give a little involuntary shudder.

No, no, no. Please, no.

I have been here many times before: the horror of seeing a child's drawing that depicts something sexual; the disclosure through drawing.

But I look again. There is something rather different about these pictures from ones I have seen children do before. These are happy, sunny, images. The colours are bright and there is a smile on the face of the main subject.

'So. Who is this man?' I ask, pointing to the figure who seems to dominate across each of the images. I don't expect an answer, although a little part of me is waiting for her to say, 'Baz,' as this seems to be the only person other than her mum who she has mentioned in her chats with Hueydewey. But we have grown used to her silences, and though I continue to ask questions in the hope that she might answer one, I am astonished when she does.

She shakes her head, then looks into the middle distance. Then her mouth opens slightly and all of a sudden one quite unexpected word pops out from it. 'Dad!'

Wow. Where did that come from? Both the act of speaking itself, and what she has said. I got the impression that Dad wasn't on the scene at all. As far as I recall, he's not mentioned anywhere in the paperwork, so I didn't even know that Eden had ever had any contact with her father. In fact, I think I understood that she had never even met him. I'll have to go back and check, now. But perhaps she hasn't. Perhaps this is some kind of idealised version of a father figure that she is creating and sketching — an exercise in wishful thinking rather than a memory of moments from the past.

Somehow, this seems even sadder.

Chapter 6

Time moves on. Eden has been with us for just over a month now.

She remains shy and extremely quiet. She still hasn't said another word to me since she said 'Dad' – though I regularly overhear her talking to Hueydewey (now homed permanently in her room by mutual agreement, after I found her trying to tug him through the kitchen one day), sometimes in the morning before I go in first thing, and occasionally I catch her whispering to the dogs – so we know for certain that there is no physical speech impediment. We don't have a diagnosis, only the doctor's reference to mutism.

In free moments I do a little research. Selective mutism is considered to be a severe anxiety disorder where someone, often a child, is unable to speak in particular social situations and contexts. We can't ignore it, because if left untreated there is the possibility that it can persist into adulthood. It's a complex condition, because it is generally considered that the child is not 'choosing' or 'refusing' to speak at certain times even though, to the untrained eye, it might seem as though there is something controlling or manipulative about her decisions not to speak.

In fact, they're literally unable to speak. They have a fear of doing it. The expectation to talk to certain people triggers a freeze response with feelings of panic, making talking actually impossible. But it is well recognised that people with this condition are able to speak freely to certain people, such as close family and friends – or, in this case, a large metal duck, when nobody else is around to trigger the freeze response. It's fairly rare, but perhaps not as rare as you might think. A form of selective mutism is actually thought to affect about one in 140 young children, though sometimes for only a short time. It's more common in girls, and among children who are learning a second language, but can also be associated with a post-traumatic stress response. In Eden's case, we really don't know what is going on; but she has been separated from her mother, suddenly, under dramatic circumstances. She is in a new space, and we must simply try to do everything we can to minimise any kind of anxiety she might be feeling – and remove any pressure on her to speak.

So, little by little, the household has developed a strange Eden-centric form of sign language in response to Eden's silence, so that they 'join in' with her. The children have begun to make shapes from their hands that sort of suggest a word or sentence. I think it emerged from the lack of verbal response originally – it is disheartening never getting a straight answer to a question. 'Would you like a cake?' has become over-performed eating movements with bloated mouths and scoffing sound effects. Eden will make the same scoffing hand movement in return to say 'yes'. It's bizarre, but it works for us, and somehow amidst all the gesture, communication takes place.

No one is ever going to describe my home as 'quiet', but it has had a knock-on effect: the decibels have been turned down a notch or two, certainly in all 'conversations' that include Eden. It all seems to have happened quite naturally. And Eden seems to get it all, every homemade bit of sign language. A proportion of children with selective mutism have developmental delays, but that doesn't seem to be the case here. There is definitely nothing wrong with her cognitive processing, whatever is going on with this selective mutism. We *all* now do these little animated actions, like we are extras in a silent movie, going through our day with overly theatrical movements and making faces. She seems to fight hard not to smile sometimes, as though she enjoys the 'game' but doesn't want to let on. When we are playing real games – cards or board games, as opposed to Vincent's digital versions – the children have become adept in choosing ones which don't require any speaking. 'Taboo' and 'Articulate' are definitely off the menu, but they find clever ways to include her in other games where she doesn't need to speak.

In these ways, I feel that we are all becoming closer. She seems more relaxed than when she first arrived, and she is not displaying any of the more challenging behaviours that other children have in the past. Her 'togetherness' makes me think she was – and no doubt still is – loved. This makes me feel happier, but I am still troubled by her silence, and wish I could understand more about what has happened to her in the past.

It is a Tuesday morning and, after the other children have gone to school, I begin to wonder what she and I can do today. Some more art? A walk? Some stories? I want her days to be full and memorable, and a whole day is a long time to fill for a school-age child. Because we have no care plan as yet, I am keeping her home initially to help give her a bit more time to settle. As a foster carer I can't make any decisions about schooling under a 'Section 20' (which is how Eden is referred to), until it goes back to court with more evidence. Section 20 refers to the Children's Care Act and just means that the Local Authority can find a home for a child without a court order when the child doesn't have somewhere suitable to live. This usually happens when there is suddenly no person available with direct parental responsibility for the child – as in this case with Ashley, Eden's mother, being in prison. Helen, Eden's social worker, has been missing in action since that first day. She hasn't made her follow-up visit, or been in touch. Daria says that she has been off on sick leave, which always makes me sad to hear. Knowing how hard it is for social workers and how much pressure they are under, it's no wonder their physical and emotional health suffers and they leave.

It's not only the personnel, but the paperwork that is holding things up. Daria is still trying to locate the missing stages of the paper trail. Sometimes paperwork just goes missing, or sometimes the social workers in the child protection team are so busy that it doesn't get written up properly at all. We only have the basics – evidence-based information about Eden – nothing helpful about her background.

These social workers work hard. They are on the front line of child protection, and sadly, since the last recession in 2008 and various changes in political priorities, many more people's circumstances have changed for the worse. With so many cuts in children's social services, the support and resources are no longer there to meet the increased demand to help children in crisis. It's usually when families are in trouble with little to no support that they crash into further difficulties, and children are taken away because their parent, or parents, can no longer meet their most basic needs. It's hard working in a system that is under ever more pressure with ever fewer resources. It's no longer a surprise that information isn't completed or goes missing. As experienced foster carers, we simply factor it into our day and get on with things.

Terry, Helen's child support assistant (that was her title the last time I looked, but it could easily have changed to something different), has been a few times, so I don't feel abandoned. My first instincts were right. She's lovely – and doesn't seem to interfere too much. She treats Eden with a grown-up attitude, which I like and admire. I've pressed

Terry for more information about who will take over from Helen, when this might happen, and what the overall plan is. She has been the consummate professional, though, and sweetly explains that she can't really divulge too much until various things have been confirmed. There are interviews lined up for a replacement for Helen, but until her post is filled there is not a lot we can get going for Eden.

In the meantime we are in a kind of limbo. Under normal circumstances I might be inclined to feel angry about this state of affairs. But actually, in this instance, there are some benefits to Eden being at home with me full time. She doesn't have to deal with the additional pressure that negotiating a new school and new classmates would bring. A further unfamiliar setting might not be helpful for her selective mutism at this stage. So, although it's controversial and we are in the very formative years of her education, where there's a danger of her falling behind her peers, I'm not pushing too hard to speed things up. She is no trouble at home, largely happy to occupy herself when she is given suggestions for activities, and the nature of my current projects means that I can get on with little bits and pieces of work here and there.

Daria is also trying to get some direction from Helen's manager behind the scenes at her end, but according to her updates, he is 'always so very busy'. Terry, in an uncharacteristic disclosure, has provided an explanation for why this might be. She has revealed that there has apparently been a sharp increase in the number of placement breakdowns with teenagers in the local area recently. She has also revealed that the authority and the police are working together to catch a group associated with County Lines, and that this is taking priority. County Lines is a term that actually denotes the mobile phone lines used to take drugs orders, but the phrase can also be used to refer directly to illegal drugs being transported from one area to another, often across police and local authority boundaries, and usually by children or vulnerable young people who have been coerced into it by organised gangs. It's maddening that it means we are pushed to the back of the queue, as it were, and all we can really do is just continue to try and shield the children from the chaos that is modern children's social care. The County Lines issue is a big deal at the moment and its impact is felt elsewhere in the system – as here, in the delay in providing a full care plan for Eden. It would be nice to know what to do about school enrolment and to be able to make plans for how long Eden will be with us, but my hands are tied for the time being. In my world, it is Eden's needs that are the most important – and so I will go on doing what feels best for now.

We have had another little breakthrough this morning: entirely unprompted, Eden has volunteered her teddy bear for the wash, tugging my sleeve so that I could watch her open the door of the washing machine and pop him in. I had resolved not to wash it at all, knowing how full of those flavours of home it must be, and I'm glad I didn't. Before he goes in the machine, she shows me that the teddy has a secret pocket, from which she withdraws a photograph. It is a picture of a man and I wonder who it might be. Baz? Her father? Of course, she doesn't tell me. Still, we have a clean, fresh teddy bear, and a relatively 'happy' and relaxed child, under the circumstances, who seems to be moving forward and apparently feeling settled in her new for-now home. When the teddy is clean and dry she replaces the photograph very carefully in its pocket. It evidently means a lot to her.

My phone goes. It's Daria, asking if she might pop round a bit later. *I've found out a few bits and pieces that will be of interest – and, good news, Eden has a new social worker. Advance warning, she may ring this morning.*

Okay, some progress. I don't envy the new social worker, though. The poor woman – Catherine, her name is – will barely have time to take her coat off before she is in her car zooming round the countryside catching up with her big backlog of statutory visits.

When Daria knocks at the door, I recognise the silhouette of her sticking-up hair immediately through the stained glass panel. She looks a little stressed. She seems rushed and her appearance is a little more unkempt than usual, but then she probably is under a great deal of pressure. I head straight for the kettle – there's no need to ask. Eden is by my side. Daria smiles to see this. She and I have had long talks about attachment and how every little tiny move in the right direction is exciting. She gives a little nod of acknowledgement and approval.

But I also know that, as fantastic a development as this is, I don't like Eden being too close when it's her that we need to talk about. I use my old technique of a lovely distraction. I get a little plate and place three cookies on it, standing a little cup of weak squash next to it (part of my gentle weaning onto H_2O during the week and saving sugary drinks for treats at the weekend). I walk with her into the garden room, through the kitchen door to the low IKEA table, and supply her with paper, pens and some books. I put some music on. She is a fan of 'The Birdie Song' from one of Lily's old pop compilation CDs. The bouncy tune has become the soundtrack to the last few weeks.

'Would you like Hueydewey in here with you?' I ask.

A smile.

I get Hueydewey from her bedroom and place him next to the table, too. I have got used to lugging him backwards and forwards and up and down the stairs so that he is around wherever she is playing. I just consider it part of my daily exercise. If she wants to be near an inanimate object – and if it's one that is going to encourage her to relax and to talk out loud – then who am I to make a judgement.

'There.'

The music is playing energetically in the background and Eden has a giant metal duck next to her – what could be more perfect?

Even though Daria is evidently in a rush with a million things to do beyond briefing me today, she understands what

I am up to and waits patiently in the kitchen while I set the scene, organising her papers and files on the kitchen table in readiness. I pull the door gently to as I return to the kitchen so that we can be seen by Eden but not overheard, just as the kettle boils. Perfect here, too.

'These are Eden's files,' she says, triumphantly, in her perfectly enunciated and very precise English, waving the papers with a flourish. 'I cannot give them to you to keep, but I can read them out to you.'

I give a wry smile. *Of course not.* Me actually reading them for myself would be too straightforward.

'Just a sec, then.' I grab some paper and a pen to make careful notes while she speaks.

'So, this Baz person. His name crops up early on in the narrative, just as you suspected.'

I learn that Baz was a former partner of Ashley's, the toxic boyfriend who effectively groomed Eden's mother, Ashley, into prostitution and drugs. She evidently became part of a dark scene that, sadly, is replicated in every city in the land.

'Baz is also now in prison,' Daria explains, 'for crimes relating to drugs.' Her mouth forms a firm straight line, lips slightly pursed, which I read as distaste. 'There is no allegation, or even suggestion, that he did anything untoward to Eden, but I know you heard Eden describe him as a "Bad Man".'

'Yes, she told Hueydewey.'

'Who knows what went on? The neighbours did submit a report that Ashley had previously been a quiet, friendly young mum who had looked after Eden beautifully until this Baz came on the scene. So, maybe he is a bad man, because he made Eden's mother change.'

What a shame. I have some sympathy for this young woman I have never met, who has ended up in prison and whose child is now part of our household.

I remember about the photograph that Eden has been keeping inside her teddy bear, and interrupt Daria's recitation to tell her.

'I don't know who it could be. Ashley was no longer in a relationship with Baz when she was arrested. And if she thinks he is a bad person, she is unlikely to treasure his picture.'

'Her dad, perhaps?'

'Maybe. But it's strange. I don't think she has ever met him. He doesn't appear in the file.'

It remains a mystery for now.

'There are some records of phone messages to the social services reporting of sex parties in Ashley's flat before she moved out,' Daria continues, with a note of disgust definitely creeping into her voice now. 'She was in a big block of flats, so different people have told about her comings and goings. There are some more reports of shouting and violence and keeping to strange hours of the day and night. It does not paint a happy picture of a place to be bringing up a child.'

She takes a sip of the coffee I have placed in front of her. 'This part here I really do not like. One of Ashley's close friends who used to babysit for Eden was one of the ones to report her concerns about the company that Ashley was keeping. It says that Eden went from being a bonny little baby to looking a bit tired, thin and dirty. I think it must be bad when it is a good friend who says these things, and not a nosy neighbour.'

'Absolutely.'

Daria goes on to tell me that Ashley is being held in a women's prison, which I already knew. 'But it is a relatively short sentence. She will be out soon. I think it was the people around her who were more culpable and received the bigger sentences – like Baz.'

Daria is right. This does not paint a very happy picture at all: a child growing up surrounded by criminal activity.

'And, wait for it, this is the big news of the day. There has been a request from Ashley to see her daughter for a contact visit.' Daria pauses for a moment. 'To take place at the prison.'

I am not surprised by this either – and am already mentally prepared for it. In fact, I am surprised that it hasn't happened sooner. It was mentioned at the very beginning because the other foster carers who were interested in Eden's referral pulled out at the point they realised that they would be expected to take Eden to the prison for contact. But I am not worried by this at all. Part of me, in fact, is looking forward to it.

When I first had Jackson and was on maternity leave, I received an invitation to undertake some part-time work in the local men's prison, a category A facility. While I naturally had some initial reservations about the project, I loved going in every Wednesday to teach art to a group of men in D wing – or, as they called themselves, the 'retirement' wing. I had such a brilliant time, and have filed it away as one of the best things I have ever done in my life. Although I was there to teach them, I learnt so much from those men. For example, one of the things they told me was that I need to listen very carefully to the news. In their position they had all day to read the papers, digest what they found there and chew the cud. Their conclusion was to feel sorry for us on the outside who didn't have time to process events and give due consideration to the government's actions at any given point. It is an interesting perspective that has remained with me for over a decade since. They trained me to take media reporting with a pinch of salt and to verify the facts of any situation. When I see people mindlessly sharing fake news on social media without doing any fact-checking for themselves, I am mindful of the wisdom of those men on the retirement wing.

No, all in all, I have absolutely no problem taking Eden to the prison for a visit with her mother. 'Actually, Daria, that would feel like an honour.'

Daria looks mildly surprised – I'm not sure that was the reaction she was expecting. But I now feel as though I am right in my earlier assumption that Ashley clearly loved her daughter and cared for her well. Initially, at least. Who knows what happened for things to degenerate in the way that they did? It sounds to me, though, as if Ashley may have been exploited – if those around her received longer prison terms than she did. She is a mother first, and has every right to see her daughter. Apart from the lack of speech, Eden has settled well – it will be good for her, too. I will be really interested to see how she communicates with her mum.

'Okay, Louise.' Daria looks me straight in the eye – perhaps to check that I am being serious.

I am also pleased that we are beginning to build a bit of a picture for Eden. It is really time to start doing her Life Story work. Perhaps we can get going on that today. I never, ever see this as a box-ticking exercise. It's so crucial that fostered children get as honest an account of their history as we can provide for them – as I know only too well from my personal experience. Growing up with no truth – or false truths – can be very difficult for a child as they make the journey towards adulthood and develop their sense of self. We all deserve to know the truth, even if that truth isn't very pretty. It's better than a fantasy.

We have taken many pictures of Eden since she first came here, in an attempt to document this important part of her life. Who knows what the next stage of it might have in store? Lloyd puts them on a CD and makes sure the social worker also has it on file. No one seems to give much thought to how to store digital imagery for fostered children, and yet it is crucial. They are entitled to their files once they reach the age of 18, and if the storage is no longer compatible by that stage then they will not have their photographs. We put copies into albums for Eden, and try to annotate them with as much detail about each precious moment as we can. We do this for all the children that we foster. But of course they are children, and by their very status, generally children who are on the move. They may have several more homes and carers, and it is easy to damage or lose these important records of their lives – hence the need for some kind of more permanent record system.

Some children have destroyed the photos of themselves out of sadness and anger – an action that they may well regret later. It is fun putting a scrapbook together and I encourage Eden to help me organise it, thinking about the order of photographs to tell the story of her stay with us. I make sure that there is a record of all the important spaces: her bedroom, the kitchen, the garden room, the garden, alongside the places we have been and things that we have done – walks to the park with the dogs, meals out. They all count: the mundane or 'everyday' moments are as important as the special occasions and treats. There is even a picture of Hueydewey the Duck next to Eden. They are really not that dissimilar in size, I notice.

We are interrupted by a phone call from Catherine, as Daria predicted, who arranges a visit for the next day. Good. Things are moving, and moving in the right direction.

The following morning I do my usual run around in preparation for a social worker's first visit. How many times have I been in this position in the past? I have lost count. I know next to nothing about this one, other than that she's new and her name is Catherine. I want to create a positive first impression. I whizz through the usual morning chores, leaving time for some additional housework and a quick clear of the hallway. Really, how many shoes and coats can a family of six possess between them?

45 minutes after the agreed appointment time there is finally a knock on the door. There has been no phone-call or text to explain the delay. It's a good job I'm working from home and can clear the decks at a moment's notice.

A tall and very slender woman with wild blonde hair jutting out in corkscrew curls stands in the doorway. The physical combination brings to mind a rag doll. I invite her in, and two steps into the hallway she goes straight down to the dogs, making a big fuss of them – almost too much of a fuss, if there is such a thing. They certainly seem to be more important than I am to her in this moment.

She is very jolly and upbeat – quite garrulous, in fact. It's as if she wants to make up for those lost 45 minutes in the first few seconds of being through the door. She tells me that she is a locum social worker who lives on the other side of the county. Her husband is a marine biologist who she sees at the weekend when she goes back to their small-holding. She must have gills or some other respiratory organ to supply oxygen, because she doesn't seem to stop for breath. While she works here during the week she lives in a caravan, north of the county, on a site with other professionals who have also had to move for their jobs. Wow, that is a lot of information about a stranger before we have made it through to the kitchen. I am almost breathless trying to listen and take it all in.

'I don't have any children of my own – my time is taken up with rescue dogs.'

Ah, that explains the rather extraordinary first-class treatment my dogs are (still) receiving. I manage to indicate with a gesture that perhaps we might move into the kitchen (I can't yet get a word in).

As we walk through she starts to compare her rescue dogs with foster children. Righto.

'They're so very similar, aren't they?'

Well, no, they're not, in my opinion, but I'm not invited to comment. She talks about loyalty and boundaries of children and animals. I decide right there and then that Catherine and I are not going to get on terribly well. I never think of these vulnerable children as sharing the traits of dogs – and I love dogs way more than most people I know.

Once I am able to prise her apart from the dogs, Catherine finally tells me the details of the plans for contact with Ashley in prison. As she speaks, my heart goes out once more to Ashley, stuck inside that place away from her beloved daughter. Poor woman. It doesn't bear thinking about. I continue to be convinced that she has been exploited in terrible ways, none of which are her fault. I try to put myself in her position and imagine what it must feel like. When I ran away from home at 15 I sailed pretty close to the wind myself, and ended up doing some things that I'm not terribly proud of. My actions were often necessary, though, and mainly a result of the fact that the only housing available to young people, as I was then, is cheap and found in dodgy areas. It is of no surprise that the vulnerable and the 'wrong-uns' live cheek by jowl. The vulnerable are preyed upon – just as I was then. Of course, I didn't realise that I was being manipulated at the time, but now that I'm older I can see all the machinations that must have been going on, and just how at risk I was. Vulnerable young women like Ashley – and my younger self – remind me of scared little rabbits who only want to be safe and warm. But the foxes have other ideas.

'As I'm sure you are aware, people need to be over the age of 18 in order to visit a prisoner. If a child is visiting, as in Eden's case, then they need to be accompanied by an adult at all times. You are happy to be that adult, I take it? You are quite sure that you don't mind?'

Why is everyone so focused on the problems with this prison visit? I assure her that I am more than happy with the arrangements.

'Well, be sure to let me know how it goes. Rather you than me,' she quips conspiratorially, as her parting shot, which I think is rather an odd, unprofessional thing to say.

When she finally departs and I close the door behind her, I am definitely glad to see the back of Catherine, and feel exhausted. Very well intentioned she might be, but she is one of those people that somehow drain away all your energy. Phew. I let out a sigh of relief, and think – a little unkindly – that maybe her husband encouraged her to apply for a job miles away.

I was very careful to make sure that Eden wasn't party to the conversation about Ashley. I'm certain that she wouldn't be able to overhear us with the door closed between the kitchen and the garden room. I have learnt not to tell a child about contact until as close to the event as possible, just in case it's cancelled and they are left feeling hurt and rejected. A child feels the loss bitterly, regardless of the circumstances of any cancellation. I have seen it all ways. I have known mothers and fathers to simply not turn up for no good reason, causing the child to feel terrible – and often somehow to blame. Sometimes all sorts of crazy things can happen when a child is that sad and hurt.

I was once involved in a serious car accident on a motorway after a child's mother didn't show and she tried to sabotage the trip by wrenching at the steering wheel. I also knew a mum who was seriously ill but never missed contact, always putting her best foot forwards no matter how much pain she was in, doing all she could to make that time special. I admired her so much. At least Ashley can't go anywhere, but there are still a number of reasons why a prison visit might be cancelled, or postponed.

But Eden seems a bit off with me, later, after Catherine has gone, and I start to wonder if she could have heard our conversation, or parts of it, after all. Catherine has a loud, shrill voice, more piercing than most, and I noticed that she was not mindful of Eden's little ears wiggling from the garden room – even though I kept my voice as quiet as I could and pulled the door shut at particularly sensitive moments. But something is going on; something has definitely upset her. She no longer wants to be as close to me as she did earlier in the day, before Catherine's visit. By the time the other children have returned from school, Eden is positively grumpy. It is quite a sight to behold, since it is all suggested through body language that seems more than usually animated and somehow 'cross' – turning her back when she is asked a question rather than the more polite shaking of the head that she might usually offer – but still no sound of her voice.

The children eat their dinner, amidst the usual stories and anecdotes that are a necessary decompression from school. I do the equally usual call for the declaration of any homework deadlines. They all offer a version of 'yes', there is work to be done – then disappear off anyway. I admire parents who can get their children to do their homework and chores straight after school, I really do. Because that is not the reality of what happens here. You never quite know how things are going to pan out. I mean, they do *do* their homework, but it's not with any of the urgency, enthusiasm and good grace that American family movies might have you believe.

I watch Eden, who seems sullen, as if she is brewing up for something. She slinks down from the table with none of her characteristic buoyancy. I am more than ever convinced that she overheard some of our conversation. I am annoyed with myself for not being more assertive with Catherine – but it was awkward. We had only just met and I didn't want to rock the boat on the first meeting – I usually wait until at least the second one for that. Besides that, I barely had the chance to get a word in edgeways.

I hear a shout, a collective shout from the boys and Lily. 'Mum! Come quick!'

I have been enjoying the peace and quiet for a while, humming my way through the washing up and the inevitable dishwasher loading, thinking, perhaps naively, that some of that mythical homework was taking place.

To my horror, what I discover is that Eden has taken both dogs and shut them in the airing cupboard upstairs. Somehow I haven't noticed that they were missing.

'I don't believe it,' says Lily, giving it her best Victor Mildrew. 'Who could do that to a poor, defenceless little dog?'

The boys, too, are furious, as they carry two whining, frightened little dogs back down the stairs.

I watch Eden while the children moan and berate her for her terrible and cruel act.

'What the hell did you think you were doing?'

'What right do you have to do something like that to Dotty and Douglas?'

'Look how terrified they are!'

Well, okay, not that terrified, I think. No real harm done. A dog biscuit soon calms them down, and drama queen

Dotty is definitely over-acting her distress. A second biscuit and they appear to have forgotten all about their 'ordeal' – their main concern being to head outside for a pee.

But Eden, of course, has no answers for them. She never speaks anyway, and she certainly isn't going to when she's under attack like this. Her eyes widen, and I think she might be about to burst into tears – but then they narrow, with no contrition, and she flees to her room. It is a discordant moment in the Allen household.

It's a worrying development in Eden's behaviour, though, as far as it goes. And an entirely unexpected one. She has been incredibly well behaved and accommodating so far. I know that all behaviour is communication, absolutely. And yes, yes, locking the dogs in the airing cupboard is a bad thing to do – but it's also a very strange thing to do when she has previously seemed so caring and so attached to them. I know that life is mucky and full of hypocrisy and misjudged choices – where fear and shame can look like anger. So what is it? What did Eden overhear? And what is she trying to tell me? I am visited by that dull light-bulb sensation once more. There are pieces of a jigsaw puzzle waiting to be fitted together, but I'm not quite there yet.

What happened to you, Eden?

Chapter 7

I need to get everyone back on track. I have some repair work to do. The dogs are fine, but Lily, Vincent and Jackson are all upset by what has happened, not to mention Eden. She must regret it. I have spoken to her and reassured her that she isn't in any trouble, but of course, she won't *tell* me what happened, or why she shut the dogs in the airing cupboard.

I need harmony to be restored. A film night, I think. Pizza, popcorn, fizzy drinks. Shared experience. Something magical and escapist, that we can all watch together. Eden's too young for any of the Harry Potter movies that touch on some dark themes. We need a nice story – one that doesn't revolve around dogs (*One Hundred and One Dalmatians* is out, then) or anything too perilous. I look at the television listings for inspiration. The first of the *Chronicles of Narnia* films is on. Perfect. An adventure story for children – a range of ages, a magical world, and Aslan, a wise and powerful lion that can speak. Eden might relate to that, given her affinity for Hueyduey and repeated attempts to communicate with the inanimate representation of a duck. Better still, the Pevensie siblings in the story fall out with each other, make mistakes and are reconciled. What could be more topical? It's made for this moment. Is the White Witch possibly too scary as an antagonist? That's my only worry. It's a PG certification, and I have a vague recollection that it begins with a bombing scene, but after that it's a fairly gentle fantasy, I think. It's Disney, for goodness' sake. How bad can it be? So, Project 'Restore Harmony' begins.

I start by knocking on Eden's door and explaining the plan. I tell her a little bit about the storyline – a magical door into another world where it's always winter, full of strange, magical creatures. She won't look at me and I can't tell whether it's shame about her earlier action, or something else. 'Do you think Hueyduey might like to come down and watch it?' I ask.

That earns a slight nod.

'Come on then, let's get him into the sitting room.' I exaggerate his weight so that she is forced to 'help' me.

'Family film night,' I announce, calling into the bedrooms of the others en route.

'But it's not even Friday!' exclaims Lily, still stroking Dotty (who is lapping up every second), and evidently still angry.

I resist pointing out that it is possible to watch a film on any day of the week.

'And anyway, I've seen the film before.'

I give her a warning look. 'You won't be wanting any of this delicious popcorn to go with it, then, will you?'

It's all the persuasion she needs. We leap into action: they know the drill. Blankets, cushions and comfort. We are soon arranged in front of the screen and the opening credits roll.

In the event, the White Witch is an irrelevance. We don't even get that far into the film.

The actress playing Lucy Pevensie looks a little bit like Eden, and she watches, transfixed, as Lucy embarks on a tour of the house while playing Hide and Seek. There is a slow-motion moment where she pulls off a sheet from a piece of furniture and it flutters majestically, while Lucy smiles up at her discovery of an enormous wardrobe. I settle further into the sofa. Here's where it all gets going, I think.

Except that Eden lets out a piercing scream, puts her hands over her ears and runs at a hundred miles an hour from the room. For a moment, I am too stunned to go after her.

'So what the hell is all that about?' says Jackson.

I am so bewildered myself, thinking exactly the same thing, that I forget to pull him up for saying 'hell'.

My mind travels back to the wardrobe incident right at the beginning. It is etched into my mind from that worried backward glance she gave to the room on the day she first arrived. She does not like wardrobes – now this with the film. And the airing cupboard – which is a little bit like a wardrobe. I rack my brains, trying to think about whether there have been any other moments like this.

There *are* other fleeting things flying around in my recollections that heighten my suspicions. Individually they are barely noticeable – which is why I haven't joined up all the dots. It's only collectively that they begin to shape a dark picture.

In spite of getting on so well with Vincent, Eden doesn't like to step foot into his room – which contains a large wardrobe on the far wall. She stands in the doorway to indicate her presence, rather than crossing the threshold. I had thought it was shyness, but perhaps it is something more. In a picture book that we read together that she enjoys called *You Choose*, a great little text that encourages its readers to decide on a fantasy life by picking friends, homes, cars, food, places and so on, she slides her hand over the wardrobe to cover it up on the furniture page. It's done with no drama or fuss – and she loves the book – but she makes the same action each time we arrive at that particular point, so I know that it's not accidental. I also sense that she knows that I know she does it, but it is just mutually accepted that that's how things are. I make no comment, and she offers no explanation.

Of course, I wish she would talk to me and open up a bit – but that's her prerogative. Really, the only word she has ever spoken to me directly out loud was when she answered the question about her drawing and said the word 'Dad' so unexpectedly. Further investigation from Daria confirms that Dad is not now, and never has been, on the scene. Perhaps it is part of her fantasy idyll – a perfect father hidden away somewhere, a bit like the characters and props in *You Choose*.

I like to mix it up a bit when making my choices, but some children pick the same things over and over again, no matter how many times they return to the book. Eden is one of those children.

So, maybe it's something to do with small spaces? What precisely is it that she is showing us? I am sure now that Catherine's loud conversation this morning was a trigger for all this behaviour. It's something to do with a wardrobe or a cupboard and something to do with her mother. I am totally perplexed.

But then the penny drops. She talked about small spaces when she spoke to Hueydewey back in the first few days of being in the house. She described sleeping in a small space like that, only big enough for her mattress. I'm sure that's what she said. I think she may have spent time shut up inside a cupboard herself. What a thing to do to a child. Poor Eden.

I head to her room. She is lying on the bed with her back to me, but no longer with her hands over her ears. That was a strange gesture. Was she trying to block out some imagined sound? She turns to look at my face as I explain that I am trying to figure it out.

'It's alright, Eden. It's fine. I understand – a little.'

Her face softens and relaxes. She was obviously worried – perhaps thought she might get into more trouble. But she is good at reading expressions, regardless of her own muteness.

'It's fine. Really. I know you can't tell me, but I think something has happened. Something to do with being in a small space, like a wardrobe.' Instinctively I reach out toward her, then remember that she will pull away.

This time she doesn't.

Chapter 8

It's contact day. I know that some foster carers would be hesitant about taking a child to see their parent in prison, perhaps having reservations about whether or not that is the right environment for a young person, but I'm not one of them. I have an attitude to life that embraces everything and attempts to meet it head-on. All experience has the potential to be life-enhancing – it's mindset, how you approach things and what you make of them that count. Our world is a messy and complicated place. I make it my business to do my best to understand rather than to judge. I don't always succeed, but I certainly try.

In spite of Eden's recent behaviours – that I am convinced are triggered at least in part by this forthcoming meeting – I feel that it is right that Eden has contact with her mother at this point. I must confess that I don't always feel this way. Sometimes I feel that contact with a parent is inappropriate at a certain delicate stage in the placement, that it has the potential to do more harm than good – particularly when a child demonstrates fear in advance of the contact – but of course I am never part of the decision-making process. In this case, however, I feel none of those things. While Eden's actions suggest a past traumatic experience involving an enclosed space, we are yet to get to the bottom of what has happened. Eden doesn't appear to display any anxiety about the visit.

All this is running through my mind as I go into the kitchen, turn the coffee maker on, and begin to gather up the ingredients for our picnic lunch. It is early – that peaceful time in the morning when I have the house to myself before the daily chaos ensues. Perhaps earlier even than usual, as I didn't sleep well last night, running through the practical logistics of today in advance. I have looked on Google Maps and found a park not too far away from the prison. My plan is to park in the prison car park and then take Eden for a walk to the park to let off some steam before she sees her mum. The prison building will be familiar that way, and Eden will be more relaxed after some fresh air and a run around. That will be far better for both of them. I always think about these contact days very carefully, aiming to leave nothing to chance.

I raid the cupboards and the fridge to place crisps, cheese straws, strawberries, blueberries, grapes, biscuits, crackers, and pork pies all out on the table. Then I go for the bread and spread along with a mixture of fillings to make some sandwiches. You name a picnic finger food and it is somewhere in the pile in front of me. I could feed the five thousand with the amount I am packing – no miracle required. Even I realise that this is somewhat over the top. But the car journey will be about three hours, and I have planned plenty of extra time so that we are able to stop for several short breaks on each leg of the trip.

I try to avoid buying food from the service stations if I can – maybe an ice cream treat on the way home, depending on how our day has gone. Though convenient, I find them ridiculously expensive in comparison to supermarket prices, so I am taking no chances on that front. I have to make the small fostering allowances go a long way, and when I have all the children with me a lunch and drinks could cost over £40. The family is very well drilled in the packed-lunch logic and routine these days.

I make my way to the sitting room where Dotty and Douglas sleep snugly in their little crate. It's very comfortable, and if I ever forget to put them in at night I hear their yaps as they sit by the door of the crate waiting for me to put them to bed. I love knowing that they enjoy their routine as much as the children. I go in and open the curtains and the top window to let in some fresh air. Their sweaty little bodies can be a bit whiffy first thing in the morning, however much I love them. I say hello to my four-legged babies, busying myself with opening up the room for the day. Douglas peers out of the cage and shakes himself down. I notice that Dotty isn't behind him; she *always* follows, ready to do her morning yoga stretches outside the crate.

She's not there!

Bewildered, I move the cushion in the empty crate, as if she could be hidden behind it.

I turn around and call her, gently at first, but then with increasing urgency. 'Dotty! Dotty! Dots!'

There is no answering patter of feet.

I begin questioning my own actions. My own sanity. Did I somehow forget to put her into bed last night? How could that have happened? I take myself back through the events of the night before. I know she was there. I *know* she was. I walk round the ground floor, full of purpose, but without direction. My heart is beginning to race as the panic mounts. At moments like this I remember how much I love my dogs and how quickly I worry for them.

I walk round the kitchen, looking in the long cupboards, opening doors and drawers. Why would she be in a drawer? I don't know, but just in case.

I go into the garden room, another one of her other favourite haunts.

Nothing.

I open the back door: I go into the garden and start calling her name.

Nothing.

I check the garden gates and the sheds. I even look inside the dustbins. I really begin to panic now. Where could she be?

Could she have been stolen in the night?

Why just one dog and not both of them? It is as if she has been spirited away. I go back inside the house and repeat the whole search scenario again, widening the parameters a little further. I check the airing cupboard, thinking of Eden's antics a few days ago, but she is not there either.

As I begin to climb the main stairs I think I detect a little 'yap', ever so faintly. So faintly, in fact, that I might be willing myself to hear something that isn't there.

I call her name once more. Another little answering 'yap'. I definitely hear it this time. I close my eyes in thanks. She is here. Somewhere.

But where *is* that sound coming from? I call her name again, listening carefully for her answer – which leads me towards the stair cupboard, a door that we hardly ever open. A little scrabbling noise. And there she is: her big round Chihuahua eyes looking up at me, very sorry and sad.

She is distressed and tired. Somehow I didn't hear her in the night, though the marks on the door suggest that she has been in there a long time and was scratching to get out. The space is surrounded by the children's shoes and coats hanging up. Maybe they helped to absorb the sound of her little pleas for help. Perhaps my disturbed sleep was something to do with her distress. I reach for her little body, and now the noises change to frantic licking and squeals of relief and excitement to be out of her dark prison.

I cradle her in my arms and head to the back door so that I can let her out for a wee. I don't know how long she has been inside here, but I imagine she must be pretty desperate. Doug comes running up, excited to see his friend. Though

I do wonder if he, with his dog logic, would actually have missed her for very long. Sometimes I have to remember that they are animals and think differently from us. I mustn't transfer human emotions onto them. I know that it's easy and it's what a lot of people do. I kiss her little face and pop her on the lawn – where she does the biggest, longest wee I have ever seen, looking up at me the whole time as if to say, 'Why, why?' There. I'm anthropomorphising again, just after I promised not to.

Unknown to me, Jackson is up, which is unusual at this time of the day. Perhaps he wants first dibs on the shower. He asks what Dotty was doing under the stairs.

'I'm not really sure. I'll ask the others when they get up.'

He looks at me and says, with an air of adult resignation, 'It was Eden, wasn't it?'

I shrug noncommittally, though it is the first thing I thought, too. Instead I say, breezily, 'I'm sure we will get to the bottom of it.' Then, changing the subject abruptly, 'Right, are you first in the shower?'

Crisis over, I make sure that the lunch and all our other journey preparations are complete before I wake up the other children for school. I pack reading books, drawing books, pens and pencils. I put my iPad in my handbag in case she wants to play a game or watch a film on the way. I like my foster children to feel that contact is a bit of a do, an event. I think it's good for them to make an effort before seeing their family. I encourage clean hair, nice clothes and a good attitude. I really don't care what their previous experience was with their parents. There is just something in me that says that foster children, indeed all children, need to get a sense of occasion and it's respectful to make an effort. You wouldn't necessarily think this mattered any more if you look at some politicians and celebrities – but it does in this household.

A child's parents may not make any effort with their appearance or with gifts for a contact visit – emotions are often running high. I have helped bake cakes, enabled and encouraged handmade cards and presents. In the past I have noticed that on the next contact the parents have usually tried a bit harder – so it works both ways. That's not going to be the case with Ashley in prison, but it will be important for her to know that her daughter is being well cared for and has made the effort for the visit.

I went shopping with Eden a few days ago for her to choose a dress. Now I get it out ready for her to put on. It's a cute little navy number with a matching headband. I'd go for something similar myself, except that this one is covered in multiple versions of Peppa Pig, and patterned with stars and rainbows. As far as I know, Eden hasn't watched Peppa Pig since she has been here; mine are too old for that, so I haven't even thought to put it on. It must be a memory or association from home. Good for her.

She had a shower and hair wash last night, and this morning I will just need to put a brush through it and clip the wild bits back.

I try once again to put myself in Ashley's position. If I was Eden's mum and I was in prison not having much fun, I'm sure that there would be plenty of time for thinking about my life. I suspect that Ashley loves Eden and did her best to care for her, but she met a man – as so many of us do – who was 'trouble'. I think women like the excitement. I know I did, once. When I was younger I preferred the men who I knew would never ask to marry me. I didn't want the responsibility. Looking back now, I guess that was linked to my weird, traumatic childhood. Thankfully that stage passed, and now I see a link between my early life choices in partners and the abuse that I had previously suffered. My early relationships were a form of continual abuse; each man ended up becoming the equivalent of my abusive adopted mother.

Enough of that. Trying to empathise with Ashley is sending me into some uncomfortable places. That's all far too deep for a sunny morning when I have a job to do. Right now, I need to get Eden and the other children ready for the day. A very big day, in Eden's case.

One door at a time, I knock. I knock in a very specific way that accords with each child's ability to wake up and get up.

Lily, hopeless at mornings as we know, requires repeated hammering before I go in and pull back the curtains. Today I throw open the window to let the fresh air in. Her room smells a little less than fragrant. One of my parenting superpowers, a highly developed sense of smell, kicks in and I detect a banana skin in the bottom of the paper bin. My suspicions are confirmed and I remove it as I pass. I hear a groan and a mumble. It is just possible that she sounds even more grumpy than usual. I have learnt not to say, 'Come on, get up,' as that simply sends her into a tizz. Instead I try, 'Morning darling, time to wake up. It's a lovely day.'

I sometimes say this even when it's grey and raining. I had a boyfriend a long time ago who, when it rained, became depressed. Sometimes he blamed me for the bad weather. I did think he was pushing his luck with that idea, and he soon became an ex-boyfriend. We live in England. It rains a lot, and even in the middle of summer we can have lingering heavy grey clouds – so I do my best to encourage an attitude where the weather is the weather, and not a form of personal persecution. When my sons were little and at nursery I remember having a conversation with the manager of the nursery about the procedure for rainy days. She explained that the children played indoors during inclement weather. I was a little agitated by this and remember repeating a quote from a now retired children's social worker whom I admired enormously. Her name was Annie and she wore a long dark red cape in the winter. One of her mottoes was, 'There is no such thing as bad weather, just bad clothing'. She wouldn't have any nonsense with plans being put off because of the weather. If any social workers, or foster carers, looked like they were being 'wet' (forgive the pun), out would come that little saying. She was absolutely right. Children need to experience all weather. I believe it's called 'being alive'.

But today the sun *is* shining.

'What do you want me to do about it?' she grunts. 'Photosynthesise?'

I go up to Vincent's attic room; he does have the best room in the house, but he is also the only child that *could* be in the attic room. Even with its sloping apexes, it is a large space and could feel isolated within the house. Vincent has always been emotionally secure and comfortable enough not to need me all the time. He likes his independence – whereas Jackson, who is older, still likes knowing I'm nearby. I always keep the foster children close by. They tend to like their bedroom doors open and a light on, for obvious reasons.

When I'm satisfied that they won't fall straight back to sleep, I head off to see Eden. Her little body is folded up tightly beneath the duvet. Though I know that she must fall asleep, she never looks entirely relaxed. I gently pull the cord of the roller blind to let the light in. She stirs slightly, so in my best Mary Poppins sing-song voice I say, 'Eden, time to wakey wakey.' She turns a crumpled face to look at me. She smiles. Then she remembers that she is emulating Lily and doesn't like getting up. I remind her of the day's events by indicating the clothes I have laid out for her. That does the trick. By the time I have helped her into her smart clothes, there is a gaggle of children collecting outside her door.

'Mum! She's been hurting the dogs!'

Oh dear. This is not a very auspicious start to the day, and it's going to take some explaining.

'Go downstairs, everyone, where we can have a chat.'

I wish Lloyd was here. He's not going to be pleased when he hears what's been going on. I leave Eden to finish putting her socks on and head down to the serious council that is taking place.

They are not happy at all.

One by one they list all the occasions where they have seen Eden put one of the dogs, usually Dotty, into a box or a cupboard. The crimes are many, and their outrage is genuine and palpable.

'It's not fair, they are so little and defenceless.'

'Why does she do it?'

'You found Dotty in the shed the other day, didn't you? With a spade wedged against the handle.'

'It's horrible! What's wrong with her?'

'Why Dotty?'

'I found Dotty in her toy box the other day, that yellow wicker thing at the end of her bed,' Lily says. 'Whimpering, trapped in there all by herself.'

I too am interested that Eden selects Dotty for this special attention. I wonder if it is because she is a girl, like Eden. I am fascinated – and alarmed by the small spaces and the way this behaviour has played out.

Someone must have locked Eden away into small places. Who? Baz? Or was it her mother? The woman that we are going to visit today? I have had a feeling all along that Ashley is not the bad guy in Eden's story, but what if I am wrong?

Before Eden walks into the kitchen I have just about managed to persuade the children to think differently. Maybe this is also connected with the fact that Eden's mother is herself in prison, trapped in a confined space. I am open and honest with them, and they can see the connection.

'And today, she is visiting her mother inside the prison. Do you notice how all of these actions with Dotty have happened since the visit has been in the calendar?'

I ask the children to try to empathise, which is a big ask, and convince them that Dotty is fine. I actually have no evidence that she is fine – she may be completely traumatised – but for now she is busy nibbling the top of her tail. Perhaps she has fleas from the long grass or the cats. There, something else to do.

At times like this, a foster carer will feel guilty. You have the needs of the foster child jammed alongside the needs of the other children. It is always a balancing act. We have to be imaginative and think fast on our feet. In this case, I resort to bribery.

'Because I'm taking Eden to see her mum today, I'll pick you up something from the service station. What's it to be?'

In chorus, they call out for a particular brand of mini cakes that come in round, plastic containers. I know exactly the ones they mean. As a working mother I am sometimes reduced to these quick, cheap fixes. Mind you, there is nothing cheap about this particular treat. It has, at least, bought me some time for now, and will maybe allow them the space to cool down from their understandable distress and blame-game.

I chase them out of the front door, calling out the checklist for the day: PE kits, trainers, water bottles, notes about a school trip, homework, money for a break-time cake sale, reminders about after-school clubs, hockey sticks, rugby boots, shin pads. Then I look around at the devastation that has been left in my kitchen. With the amount of cereal and toast that has been consumed, it's like a swarm of giant human-sized locusts have been through. Most mornings I feel like I've done a day's work by the end of breakfast time.

Just Eden is left. I don't want to ruin her day, but I can't let what has happened, and what I now know about all the other times it has happened, go unchecked. I have a responsibility – both to a beloved family pet and to the other children.

'I found Dotty in the cupboard under the stairs,' I tell her, with a questioning eyebrow.

She looks back at me with a quizzical stare, as if offering a question in return.

I do suspect that her emotional intelligence is a bit wonky, and I remind myself that she is still so very young. I know that it will be hard to admit to what she has done.

'It's okay,' I tell her. 'Nothing bad has happened. Happily, Dotty is fine.' I allow that to sink in. 'But when I found her she was very scared, and she was shaking.'

Shaking in a way that is not strictly Chihuahua, and has worried me greatly, but I don't say that. I collect up the bowls that – surprise – didn't make it to the dishwasher, and bring out a fresh cereal bowl from the cupboard to begin pouring from Eden's favourite packet.

Against that sound of the flakes falling against the china of the bowl, Eden says, 'They locked me in the wardrobe.'

When a child makes a disclosure you never have a pen and paper to hand. You're usually driving, or with your hands in the sink washing up, or – like now – decanting cereal. I seem to have vastly overfilled the bowl, and flakes are now falling onto the kitchen table.

She stays focused on the spillage as I remind myself to stop pouring.

'Darling, you know that no one should have locked you in a wardrobe or anywhere. That's not how we look after children.'

Eden opens her mouth. Miracle of miracles, are we about to have a second whole sentence out loud?

But just as she goes to speak, my phone rings. I see Catherine's name flash up. I can't believe that woman! Her timing is terrible. I let it ring. What was Eden about to tell me?

'Eden, I would love to hear more – I am here to listen to what you have to say, but I had better listen to what Catherine has to say first – in case it's something to do with today's visit.'

Eden stares into her cereal bowl.

My phone pings to show that Catherine has left a message.

I head into the garden room and dial the messaging service. 'Louise, it's Catherine. It's urgent. Can you call me back immediately, please?'

I don't like messages like this. There is a seriousness to Catherine's tone that I haven't heard before and is entirely unsettling. Something is very wrong.

I turn back to Eden with a smile. 'I'll be back in a minute. Whatever you do, don't crush your Frosties into a paste again, will you?'

This is very calculated on my part. She's done it before, and actually, I'm saying it to remind her. If I say not to do it then she will – and that will occupy her for a few more minutes while I am on the phone. I go beyond the garden room and walk out into the garden itself so that Eden can't hear or see me. She might have great lip-reading skills. You would be amazed at some of the unacknowledged skills that traumatised children can develop.

I find Catherine's name to return the call. It only rings once before her voice is on the other end, slightly breathless.

'Thanks for calling me back so quickly, Louise. I'm afraid I have some tragic news. Are you sitting down?'

I steady myself into the garden bench, just as something seems to fall away from the pit of my stomach. I know that all of my children are safe and well – I have waved them off just a few moments ago. Lloyd is working away again, but he has texted me already to say that he is enjoying his hotel breakfast. He even joked that it was nice to be able to locate a spoon for his coffee. I know that he is fine.

'It's Ashley. Eden's mum. There's no easy way to say this. I'm afraid that she was found dead in her cell this morning.'

'Dead?'

'Yes, I'm sorry. They believe it was suicide.'

I have no words. I can't believe what I am hearing.

'Louise, are you there?'

That poor child.

'Yes, yes, I'm still here. Thank you for letting me know.' My speech is inadequate. I have resorted to some kind of auto-pilot setting. I hang up, and remain on the bench, retreating into a quiet state.

What has happened with Dotty this morning feels like a total irrelevance. I feel so much warmth and love for poor Eden right now that I think I might burst.

Chapter 9

The day falls apart.

The world around me comes crashing down. I turn around to look at Eden and my head goes into a spin. I watch her face – innocent of the devastating news I have just heard, and that she will have to hear very soon. She is playing with her bowl of cereal, exactly as I warned her not to, no doubt excited about the day ahead, with no idea of the tragedy and sadness that is about to hit.

I step into the kitchen and move the picnic to one side. I can't face putting it all away – and anyway that feels wrong somehow, as though it would be in some way disrespectful. It's an awful lot of food. I will think about that later.

My mind turns to Ashley, a woman I have never met but feel all kinds of sympathy for. This is all so very, very sad. A young woman, all alone in prison, away from her baby girl. I know that Ashley loved Eden, I just know it, somehow. I tell myself that I could feel it. I'm sure of it.

I don't have any details. I don't know how she did 'it', the thing I can't bring myself to say, but I'm guessing it was an overdose of some sort. I don't know why I think that, but I consider that if that is the case, then she would have had to have organised herself over a period of time, to acquire the number of tablets she would need. That level of premeditation is too awful to think about. Why is my mind doing this? Perhaps it was more spontaneous. Maybe she hanged herself, or maybe cut herself. But in prison, those two ways would also require a degree of preparation. Oh my God, it is too terrible to think about. I wish I knew more about what happened, and at the same time I'm glad I don't.

The poor prison officers who found her, I think next. When Jackson was a baby and I had my time working in the men's lifers' prison, I remember that the men and the guards on the whole seemed to have a good relationship, what seemed like a warm relationship in many cases. Many of the guards were ex-service personnel and maintained a kind of camaraderie with their charges. Some of the prisoners were also ex-services. I saw their cells. I saw how they lived in prison with reduced privacy – and fears of trouble from other prisoners or a bad guard.

But I was made aware quite quickly that the prisoners feared the prison psychologist more than anyone else in the hierarchy of prison life. If the psychologist walked by, the men became different; they adjusted their behaviour almost as if to negate themselves, to make any sense of personality disappear.

They behaved like robots with their heads down, drawing on the paper, totally absorbed to all intents and purposes. When I asked them why they behaved this way, one said, 'Never trust the psycho.' I thought he was just being witty and it was a throwaway remark, but he meant it. Another one of the men, a man called David, who was found guilty of murdering his wife in a crime of passion, explained.

'The psychologist puts words into our mouths. She looks for things that aren't there.'

He recalled a time when he had been caught sitting day-dreaming, miles away from his prison cell in his head, looking absently across the room. He later saw what she had written down: *David is having suicidal thoughts.*

They really didn't like it or like her – and considered it a form of gaming to keep their real thoughts hidden from her. I wonder about Ashley, for whom it worked the other way. She must also have kept hidden how she was feeling, but truly was having suicidal thoughts. I return to her youth. She was so young, too young, the same age as my oldest stepdaughter. How could she have kept those suicidal thoughts hidden from whoever was assessing her inside?

I know what it's like living in a city, being that age. I can only imagine that for a young woman, a single mum on her own, that life would be pretty tough. When I was a younger woman I would walk to college in the mornings or saunter through town looking at the young mums pushing their buggies – looking stressed and unsupported – and think,

'Not for me.' Without a supportive family and network of friends around you, life with a baby can be grim. I look at Eden who, through all her silence, is simply beautiful. Traces of her mum must run through her. I've never seen a picture of Ashley. I hope I do. I would love to see if Eden has her looks, or whether they all come from Eden's father. My mind is going in all these strange directions. Blimey. What a mess.

Lily, perhaps remembering her own situation, sends me a quick text message wishing me luck for today with the contact visit. I don't tell her the detail, but just say there's been a problem at the prison and that Eden is here today with me. I keep it light. What else can I do? She and the boys will be respectful, I know, but will soon sense that something far greater is going on. For now it can wait. There will, of course, be a ripple effect on the whole household.

Lloyd is away again for the time being. I could do with the support of him being here to help me handle this, but he is involved in setting up at a big trade fair this week that is taking him away for multiple meetings that require overnight stays. He left yesterday evening for this business trip and won't return until tomorrow. I will text him later this evening when there is time for a proper chat. Not yet. It's not nice news to hear at any time. There's no need to ruin his day. I know that, like me, he will worry for Eden. Of course we all will. Eden is an innocent little girl who we have all come to care deeply for over the last few weeks – whose life has been so difficult lately, and has now taken an even more tragic turn.

My mind darts around in uncontrollable circles of thought. What a terrible shame. What an utter waste of a life. What a tragedy for Eden, left behind to cope alone in the world. How did this happen? How did it get to this stage? How did poor Ashley become so involved with the wrong people that she could end up taking her own life? How on earth will little Eden respond when she is given this sad news?

It is not for me to do the telling, but it will be up to me to handle the fallout. I feel like howling out loud. Then I think about how I am going to find a way to help her understand that her mummy loved her, but sadly her life's journey took her to some dark places. I wonder how many other young women get caught up with men like this Baz. How does this happen? I have never met the man, and only heard his name spoken out loud by Eden talking to a metal duck, but I blame him for what has happened. It is easier to have someone to blame for what feels so senseless.

And now, instead of a long car journey and a prison contact visit, I'm expecting a double visit from Daria and Catherine. At least there will be plenty of food, I think, eyeing the picnic that I don't really know what to do with. I am certain that Daria will be a model of professionalism and kindness, and will help me to help Eden deal with this. Catherine, on the other hand, I consider to be a bit of a loose cannon. I sense that I will have to monitor *her* and be careful of how she is around Eden – which is not the way it should be at all. Technically, it's for Catherine, as Eden's social worker, to tell Eden that her mummy is dead. I wonder if she has had to do anything like this before. What a nightmare we are all caught up in.

I'm not sure I can do this. I want to be anywhere but here, looking at this picnic, and at Eden with her cereal bowl, who doesn't know about the devastating blow that is about to strike.

Somehow I carry on. I prepare to busy myself. It doesn't matter with what. I take a deep breath, several of them. I clatter about with kitchen things in an attempt to prepare for the rest of the day. It's not a situation that anyone can be prepared for, but I can do some practical things. I feel the need to get cups out ready for the visitors, place spoons on saucers, get tea and coffee jars out, and sort which of the packets of food can be used to entertain two social workers. I can't bring myself to speak. Usually I chatter away and make enough conversation for both of us, but not today. I will myself to say something – anything – so that she doesn't guess.

'Are you done there?' I manage, making sure that I am turned away from her as I ask.

Eden pushes the bowl away in answer. She gets down from the table and positions herself on the floor so that she can 'talk' to Douglas more easily. Douglas has his paw on her shoulder. In this sad moment, knowing what I know but she doesn't, it seems a peculiarly human gesture.

It nearly does for me.

Eden is smiling and looks relaxed and contented. For now. I can't imagine how this next conversation is going to go and how much more of her world is going to shatter. We had a tempered glass garden table that broke into what seemed like a million pieces when we tried to move it, once. The pieces kept on cracking, even after the damage was done, splintering exponentially. The noise went on like fireworks, long after the initial break, in a chain reaction of sound. The idea of the toughened glass is to create 'pebbles' so that they aren't dangerous, but there were just so many of them. I wanted to stop and rewind time back to a point where the accident hadn't happened and the glass tabletop was still intact, not in these countless still-shattering pieces. It might have been a safety mechanism, but it still took what felt like hours to clear up, and we ended up having to vacuum up tiny shards from amongst the grass in the garden; there were too many and they were too small to pick up or sweep away. I don't want Eden to break like that. I wish I could rewind time and stop Ashley, a woman I have never met, from doing what she has done, and prevent the pain from coming to Eden.

I bring Hueyduey downstairs and put him out in the garden. It's a nice day. How dare it be a nice day? He will be a distraction when Catherine and Daria come.

Somehow, time passes. I fill the rest of it with needless, mind-numbing activities until later, when the doorbell goes. The noise is shocking, a shattering sound from reality, even though, as on the day that Eden first arrived, I am expecting it.

First up it's Catherine, still rag-doll-like in her demeanour, arms and legs seeming to fly about uncontrollably as if they are only pinned to her body by a thread. She is laughing too loudly as she stands at the front door. I am sure that the laughter is nervous, but I issue a silent prayer to anyone who might be listening that she can just get herself under control.

Next comes Daria, just behind her – calm and measured, even more so by contrast. I let both women in to the house. Catherine starts talking about the traffic and the parking and things that simply don't matter. She is filling awful space with disconnected words, and I don't blame her. I realise, though, that I'm not actually sure if these women have met before. You never know who knows who in children's social care. I'm guessing that maybe Catherine's reputation precedes her.

In they come.

Reality marches on.

The dogs start barking in a belated show of 'guarding' the house and Eden stands up to see who is here. She presents her 'welcoming' face to the visitors – she is always so accommodating. All I have told Eden so far is that there have been some changes of plans to our day and that the social workers are coming – but as most mums will tell you, it's never possible to be quite sure what's gone in. 'Now you've said hello, you can leave us to it and play with Hueydewey for a little while, if you like?' I say, knowing that Eden will be itching to get away from this group of adults and the pressure that might be put upon her to speak. 'I've put him out in the garden so that he can get some sun.'

Eden scampers off and I wait for the two women to settle themselves down. I put on the kettle. I have nothing to do, as I laid out all the cups, saucers and spoons ages ago. So I look at Catherine. Nothing about her demeanour fills me with any confidence about how she is going to handle this most delicate of moments in a child's life. I decide there and then to take a bit of control − after all, it's my house.

I look at Catherine directly. 'Right. So, how are you going to do this?'

Daria also turns to look expectantly at Catherine, who, in turn, looks blankly back at her, and then at me. It could be part of a choreographed comedy sketch if it weren't such an awful situation.

'I don't actually know. I was hoping you would have some ideas?' At least she has the decency to lower that shrill voice as she says it.

My inner voice seethes quietly, *For God's sake, woman! Take control of this. You're meant to be in charge here.* My actual, outer voice says, 'Are you going to tell her, Catherine?' I want to put the emphasis on that 'are', but fear that it will sound too challenging.

Catherine looks at Daria for support. Perhaps even as if to say, *Can you do it?*

I quickly make a decision. I don't trust Catherine to handle this. Or not to handle it well, at least. If Catherine tells her, there is every chance that she will do it badly and potentially make matters worse for Eden. That's if they could be worse at all.

Out loud I say, 'Who feels most comfortable?'

There is a silence. Not a tumbleweed silence, but a tense one. Daria looks at me. I look at Catherine. Catherine looks at the floor.

I am actually becoming rather cross. 'Have you not already had this conversation?' I pipe up.

Daria looks at Catherine. 'It's officially your job, as you know. But it's not an easy one, as we all understand. I don't want to tread on anyone's toes, but if you would rather, I can do it. I have spoken to Eden a few times now. She knows who I am.'

Catherine reaches for a biscuit. A biscuit? I know I have put this food out, but I don't expect anyone to really eat it under the circumstances. 'Yes. That would work,' she nods.

I keep my thoughts to myself.

Daria gets up and moves into the garden room towards Eden, who is sitting on the lawn in the sunshine next to Hueydewey.

I follow, but stay just inside the door of the garden room so that I'm not intruding.

Catherine waits in the kitchen with the biscuits. I want to interpret this as giving them space, and my better self manages to.

Daria positions herself near Eden, not too close to feel invasive. She reaches into her bag and pulls out a children's book. She asks Eden to help her read it. It's the story of a rabbit who dies.

Oh my, I feel so sad. My eyes start welling with tears as I watch this delicate, painstaking, well-considered scene play out before me. Daria is amazing. She is rapidly turning into my favourite ever social worker. I have liked her from the start, but now I watch true professionalism in action. She is one of the ones who boldly puts the child before the paperwork, instinct before bureaucracy. I'm glad that she is taking on this role, and not Catherine. I have met many brilliant social workers but Daria is in another league.

I sit quietly on the old IKEA chair – a piece of furniture that has seen much better days, but the children love it and refuse to let me throw it out. Daria gently explains that Mummy, like the rabbit, has died.

I watch Eden's face try to understand, try to process the unprocessable. She hasn't spoken. Not even this news is encouraging any of her words to fall out. I have some kitchen roll in my hand and soak up the salty tears gathering on my own cheeks.

From my vantage point I look back into the kitchen and watch Catherine scrolling on her phone. How, I'm not sure. I'm not sure about that one at all.

I move forwards so that I am nearby if Eden needs me. Daria remains next to Eden as she absorbs the information. She picks up the book and begins to look at the pictures again, going back over the story she has just heard. My heart is breaking. Eden looks at me and her expression is puzzled. She looks really bewildered, as though she is trying to understand but can't. I'm worried that she is really confused and maybe needs to have the news explained again.

Daria manages to give off an aura of being entirely relaxed in our company, in this moment. She looks sad, but is holding herself together as the consummate professional she is. I suspect that she will sit in her car and have a cry later. You'd have to be inhuman not to.

Eden closes the book and gets up from the grass.

Our eyes follow her. She walks slowly round the garden, turning this way and that, directionless. She goes up to the window of the garden room and looks inside, then back out to the garden. Our eyes continue to follow her. My instinct is to run up and hug her, but we can never force our hugs onto children.

I feel useless.

Eden walks towards me, and then puts her head into my neck. Every part of me aches, and tears are flowing freely down my face as I put my hand gently on the back of her head. Her soft hair sticks in my fingers.

I look across at Daria, who is now crying too.

Eden stands there for what feels like an eternity, breathing into my neck, her little body hot with grief as she begins to take it in. Slowly I move my other hand over across her back and with the lightest touch I can muster, I hold her. She just stands there neither resisting the embrace, nor falling in for more. It is a moment that I will never forget. She feels whole and warm, but I wonder if she is cracking into little pieces, splintering inside.

The atmosphere is quickly burst by Catherine, who steps into the garden.

'Would you believe it? I need to talk to you. They can't find—'

Even in these circumstances I can register that Daria's face is an absolute picture. Her usual, professional, deadpan face (that, yes, a moment ago was quietly weeping) is now replaced with an expression of utter fury.

'Thank you, Catherine.' Daria cuts her off. 'We'll be there in a *minute*,' she hisses through gritted teeth that she makes no attempt to disguise.

I pick Eden up and put her squarely on my lap now. Every maternal instinct is telling me to just keep Eden safe – and that's from insensitive social workers, as well as the cruel world.

Daria stands and dusts herself off from the grass, returning through the garden room back to the kitchen to talk to Catherine. She carefully closes both doors behind her so that Eden will not be disturbed by whatever nonsense Catherine felt was worth interrupting us for. I am grateful for these small but important considerations; Eden does not need to hear this, whatever it is. I continue to sit with her, my arms fully round her little body. We can sit here all day if needs be. I feel only a maternal love, in its purest form, and a powerful desire to protect this girl, struck by tragedy. My head has finally stopped spinning as I hold this little poppet, an innocent five-year-old child in care whose mother has died under the most dreadful of circumstances. I feel more, perhaps irrational anger towards 'Baz', whoever he may be. It must be his grooming and manipulation of Ashley for his own perverse gain that has left this child without a mother.

How can you do that to another human being? My usually liberal tendencies have evaporated. I hope he stays in prison forever.

Chapter 10

Daria calls at 7 am. I wake up to the ringing sound of the mobile after a terrible sleep. I was awake all night, thinking about Eden and what happens next. I haven't had conversations with any of the family yet, but I'm wondering if we could or should step up and put ourselves forward to be her long-term carers – or even adopt her. I adore this child; she deserves better. Her mum deserved better. I sit up in bed, rub my eyes and say hello to Daria. I think about trying to disguise my sleepy voice for a moment, but decide against it.

'Blimey Daria, don't you ever sleep?'

She laughs and says, in her lilting Eastern European accent, 'I'm un-fire today, Louise.' The 'r' of 'fire' is rolled out as if to emphasise her purpose and determination even more.

I do like Daria, even more so since her performance in breaking the sad news to Eden, and I think that if she leaves her locum role here then I would love to stay in touch with her. She has a good energy and enjoys getting things done: a breath of fresh air into the children's social care system that likes to say 'No' or 'Can't' at almost every opportunity. Not Daria. She does not understand 'can't'.

She explains that in spite of Catherine's untimely interruption two days ago (which was to let us know that they hadn't been able to track down Eden's father yet, a man called Matt – I am still infuriated by that inappropriate barging in; important, yes, but not important enough to interrupt two adults consoling a grieving child), they have now been able to trace him.

'My manager is being very supportive of the idea that we meet Matt together. I have gone ahead and made an appointment with him for later this week, on Thursday, at the office. I hope that was the right thing to do – that it is ok with you and you can come here.'

Whatever was happening on Thursday can be rearranged. I love the speed with which she has achieved this.

'It was all decided at a professionals' meeting,' she tells me, pausing to let that sink in. 'I'm sorry.'

It is not her place to apologise, but I appreciate it.

These 'professionals' meetings' are usually held without the foster carer's knowledge or invitation and can result in bad feeling, mainly because it's the foster carer who knows the child best. It is a bureaucratic managerialist system where managers can tell social workers how to think. Daria knows that I know this, and I also know that she, like me, disapproves. I have seen her roll her eyes in the past when she has to deliver the corporate message to us. I picture her doing it now at the other end of the phone line.

'There is more.'

Every now and then foster carers receive a request to think about converting a foster placement into an adoption or Special Guardianship (SGO). It feels like when you go to the hairdressers' and they try to upsell hair products. Most foster carers politely say, 'we'll think about it.' I'm not comfortable with the level of marketing that goes on around looked-after children. It can sometimes feel as though they are seen as commodities – as indeed are foster carers – to be traded and priced. When we're asked to think about changing from foster carers to SGO or adopters, my community of foster carers WhatsApp each other to ask whether we've been given the 'sales chat'. We know that ultimately it's a money-saving exercise, and any new offer may not be what it says on the tin.

'I think that Matt could be the best option for Eden. Long term. So, we have two days to put together as much information as we can about Eden's past and situation. It is enough time.' It isn't, but this is Daria's can-do attitude.

'Have you spoken to Matt yourself?' I ask.

'Yes. But only on the telephone. He was deeply saddened by the news of Ashley's death and would like to go to the funeral with Eden – although of course, things are not quite that simple.'

Like everything in children's social care, this will require some consideration. Eden is now, to all intents and purposes, a ward of the state. My understanding is that Eden has not had regular contact with her father thus far. I agree that if Matt is a good man and truly wants to look after his daughter, that will be the best outcome for her – far better than the other options I was turning over in my brain last night. But I wonder why he hasn't been involved in her story so far. And I just hope it can all be done carefully. That's why I need Daria on the job – over Catherine, who I think could easily unravel the sensitive work that we are doing. It's just very annoying that she happens to be Eden's social worker.

I write down the important information from Daria, transferring the date and time of the meeting with Matt to the calendar and reassuring her that I will be there. I head down to the kitchen quietly and switch on the coffee machine, before letting the dogs out – safely where they should be this morning.

Back in the kitchen the coffee machine is doing its thing. It remains one of the best investments we made when Lloyd and I both decided to work from home. I wait for all the digital shapes and numbers to stop flashing, then place my coffee cup under the two spouts and wait for the coffee to come. I'm going to need a few more of these to get me going today. I hate the 'night chatter', when my brain goes round and round in circles and endless permutations and disturbs my rest without achieving anything. I know that it's actually pointless. I wish I had the ability to switch it off and send myself back to sleep. Coffee is going to have to work its magic today.

I'm so worried for Eden. She is not like many of the other children I have looked after in the past. Yes, she has experienced trauma, that's for sure – but she also experienced love and good parenting from her mum. She has not got the attachment issues I experience with some of the children that pass through this household. She is, on the whole, a happy little girl – or was, until the devastating news about her mother. The only thing that really marked her out prior to this was her reluctance to talk out loud. I have experienced violence and violent reactions from children – and that can be terrifying for all of us. Not little Eden. She carries herself well, in spite of the burdens she bears. I suspect that she is far more knowing than we think. More adult than her years. I know her well enough now to be able to read her face to see her eyes flicker and the corners of her mouth rise a little or turn down if she feels unhappy. Because of the lack of verbal communication, I'm far more attuned to her mood from the subtleties of her body language. She has borne her grief remarkably over the last 48 hours. But who knows what today will bring?

I tiptoe around as I get the others up and ready for school. I will let Eden sleep on. Sleep is a good healer – I know, because I didn't get much of it myself last night and I am feeling it this morning. I have this deranged idea that because I was awake worrying about her, she will be tired and need more sleep.

We are a subdued household. I don't need to tell anyone to keep their voices down. Jackson thinks about flaring up when his preferred cereal packet is empty, and

Vincent's bowl is brim-full, but thinks better of it and opts for something else instead.

The morning continues to pass smoothly once the older children have all left for school. I stack the dishwasher, rinse out the coloured glasses in the sink, fold up and hang the tea towels over the rail on the cooker, and go through the motions of an ordinary morning.

I check the kitchen clock. I think it's probably time to wake up Eden.

As I walk upstairs, I am closely followed by Pablo Picasso, my handsome black cat. His presence is reassuring. Perhaps he can sense the melancholy in the house.

I gently tap on Eden's bedroom door, and then, when there is no answer, push it open.

She's not there.

Don't panic, she can't have gone far, the logical part of my brain tells me. I walk into the other rooms along the hallway, calling her name in my breezy 'sing-song' voice. I keep moving along the rooms until I get to the guest room, right at the other end of the landing. The door is slightly ajar, though I usually keep this one closed. I open the door further. No sign of Eden, though. Then I notice that the door to the wardrobe is also open a crack. It is a French antique, a monstrosity of a thing.

Inside I keep spare blankets and hang up our heavy winter coats with lavender bags attached to the hangers. What could she possibly want in there? I let her know

I'm coming. I call, 'Eden.' When I carefully pull the door open fully I see little Eden, cowering in the corner of the wardrobe, sitting on some blankets with her hands over her head, crying. It is a picture of misery.

I feel devastated.

I crouch down and reach out for Eden's hand, stroking it gently with my index finger.

'Hello, darling, I've been looking for you. I'm glad I've found you. What are you doing in here?'

She doesn't look at me but at my finger stroking her hand. She points upwards, fearfully, to the ceiling of the wardrobe.

I see a crack of light shine through, from the gap between the wooden boards, nothing more. She begins to shiver, as though she is ill. I wonder if she has a temperature. The quiet little sobs begin again.

My brain is in overdrive. Why is she in here? It could be a safe space, but I don't think it is. And yet she has come here voluntarily. If only she would talk, tell me what was the matter, what it is that's going on inside that little head. I've been tiptoeing round these issues. I need to get to the bottom of what has been going on. I watch her whole body stiffen as I say, 'Did mummy have a wardrobe?'

She nods.

'Did you play in mummy's wardrobe?'

She shakes her head.

I continue with another question. 'Do you feel sad inside this wardrobe?'

A nod. Stating the bleeding obvious, Louise, but it feels like a game of 20 questions and I need the 'yes' answers.

'Did something happen inside a wardrobe that scared you and made you feel sad?'

She nods. I feel a little sick.

'Did you get stuck inside a wardrobe?'

A shrug. It's not as affirmative as the other 'yes' responses, but it's not a 'no'. What does that mean?

I follow her eyes as she looks up at the ceiling once more.

'Have you ever been locked up in a wardrobe?'

A return to the nods.

Keep going, Louise, keep going.

Years ago, I heard of a story – I think it was from a film, but it could have been one of those urban myths that go round when people are telling stories on a sleepover or around a campfire. I'm not a fan of horror films, and if you knew more about my own troubled childhood you would understand why. I do remember a group of students, younger than me, talking about a girl who was locked in a cupboard and tortured from the outside by a pair of sadistic captors. Maybe they were talking about a horror film they had seen at the cinema. Whatever it was, it sounded hideous – and exactly the sort of thing I would have avoided like the plague. They pushed things through the woodgrain and she never knew where the next torture was coming from. Knives, boiling tar, rats. I think it ended with them flooding the cupboard with water so that she drowned. I have tried not to think about it ever since, but it pops into my head now from the way she keeps looking upwards at the crack of light from the top of the wardrobe, and I take a punt.

'Was there something in the wardrobe with you?'

A shrug. It doesn't mean 'no', I think now, but I'm not quite on the right track.

Her eyes move upwards once more.

'Did something come in from the top of the wardrobe?'

She nods again, eagerly this time.

'Did someone pour something – water on to you?' I hazard.

A nod. And a swallow. This 'conversation' is very hard for her.

'Was it an accident?'

I know, before she gives me the headshake, that it wasn't.

She has stopped crying, the sobbing at least, but tears still run down her cheeks as she reaches down and slowly inches up the legs on the Peppa Pig pyjamas she favours. She points at the faint redness there. I had noticed the marks when she was in the bath shortly after she first arrived, but they were faint and hadn't really registered properly. I thought they were old insect bites. Nothing to worry about. Now that I look more carefully, and with a possible context that part of me doesn't want to acknowledge, I realise that they could very well be faded water burn marks. Why wasn't I more attentive in the beginning? I am usually, but Eden had the demeanour of someone better cared for than a number of the placements we have looked after, and I must have been blindsided by that. It's not like me. I will have a much closer look when she has a bath later. But this is terrible, and amounts to disclosure.

I have to report this to Catherine and Daria.

'Well, nobody is going to hurt you here. I promise you that. You are safe.'

We need normality, whatever that might be. I try to entice Eden out of the wardrobe with the idea that we could make some ginger biscuits – she likes those. 'But I need your help to do the mixing. I won't manage by myself.'

I can feel my work plans disintegrating, and moving further and further away from realisation. I know I will be burning some midnight oil over the next few weeks trying to catch up. I have a book deadline looming, but it will just have to wait. My agent knows what I write about. She'll understand that I'm living a bit of it at the moment. I help Eden out of the wardrobe and now she doesn't resist. I reach out with one arm and she takes my offer of a hand. In spite of the terrible circumstances, my heart gives a little skip.

When we get downstairs I feel the conflict of dealing with social workers to report what I have just heard, or looking after my precious ward. I choose Eden. The bit of paper can wait.

I open the big bottom drawer by the kettle to find a baking tray. The drawer makes a loud noise on its runners and Eden looks up. But she is looking above the drawer, at the kettle itself. In fact, her eyes make a little darting movement towards it, as if she is trying to direct my attention.

'What is it? What do you want to tell me? Are you looking at the kettle, Eden? Was it water from a kettle that was poured through the cracks in the wardrobe?'

She nods, and I feel sick again. That is hideous. Who would do that to a child? I am guessing that this was Baz's fine work, though I have no evidence for it. So I ask her directly if Baz hurt her.

She nods once more, but the gesture is accompanied by a rare little word this time. She says, 'Lucky.'

I would love to know what's lucky about having a bad man pour boiling water over a little girl. What kind of warped world is this? How can she conceive of that as being in any way lucky? I shake my head.

I direct her attention away from the kettle and towards the pictures in the recipe book. 'We don't have to make ginger biscuits. We can make whatever you want. You choose.'

We both pore over the images as we turn the pages. It always amuses me how people make such joyfully appreciative sounds when they look at food – and little Eden is no different. I love it. She looks at a picture of a chocolate cake and makes an elongated 'mmm' sound.

That clinches it. 'Right, well we'll do that one then!' I check the cupboard. 'After we have been to the shops to get some of the ingredients.' I know it's really important that we teach our children to cook and learn life skills, but some of the ingredients for the recipes cost a small fortune. Today, though, that expense seems irrelevant, and a quick run to the shops is another distraction.

Back from our dash to fetch the groceries, I set out the ingredients on the butcher's block. I place down my large mixing bowl and drag the stool over from the corner with my foot while I tie an apron round Eden. I show her how to stand on the stool to reach the bowl. We carefully measure out each element and pour the ingredients into the bowl. I start blending the butter and flour until it's soft enough for Eden to feel that she is now the chief cook. She is happy now, and I can hear deep heavy breathing from her intense concentration. It's a lovely sound and sight. Eden chooses the Christmas tree cutter, which makes me smile, as I joke about it being Christmas all year long. Sometimes, with Eden, you forget that she doesn't talk. Her body language and facial expressions tell me everything I need to know – apart from what Baz did.

I want to get to the bottom of why she thinks being hurt – either by accident or as a form of abuse – is somehow 'lucky'. It's such an odd thing to say. While the sponge halves are baking, I set up the TV in the garden room. It's a ritual for me to set activities up for the younger children. I wonder if it's to do with my previous life of teaching. I like to feel that I have explained myself and that they understand. She sits back on the sofa, suddenly surrounded by dogs and cats, and Hueydewey of course, and watches a stream of children's television. I have deliberately created this window of opportunity to be able to call Catherine and Daria about the wardrobe disclosure.

I am just about to call Catherine – who technically should be first in line as Eden's appointed social worker – when I decide to call Daria first. I continue to see Catherine as a wild card – her behaviour has shown me that Eden is not always front of centre in what she does. She is not what Eden or I need right now. After I have spoken to Daria, I promise myself that I will call Catherine as a matter of protocol. I get hold of Daria straight away (this is another revelation – she seems always to pick up). Daria is on her hands-free set in her car, on her way to a teenage placement breakdown. She listens to my report and shares my intrigue as to why Eden would think any of what happened to her was lucky.

Daria goes quiet on the other end of the phone for about three seconds – long enough for me to think that we might have lost connection as she moves through areas with less reception. Then says what sounds like, 'Lockey'.

'What?'

She repeats, 'Lockey. Not lucky. Maybe you mishear.'

For a moment I think Daria has gone slightly mad, or her faultless English has somehow betrayed her.

'Sorry? What is Lockey?'

'Lachie. L-A-C-H-I-E.'

I am none the wiser for this.

'Lachie is a person, Louise. A very bad person. A criminal person, in fact.'

Daria goes on to explain that she was up late last night with the police report from the child protection team. She has a friend in the team who suggested she took a look at it. Lachie was the boss, the ringleader of the criminal gang that resulted in both Baz and Ashley going to prison.

I love Daria's accent. She makes it sound like a dialogue from a film. The last few days have had an air of unreality about them anyway.

'Can you remember and write down everything that Eden said?' Daria asks. 'And send it to me by email, please, Louise.'

What she tells me next begins to sound increasingly like a fictional outline of a gangster film. Baz and his fellow gang members would take it in turns to 'cop to it' and do time for Lachie, for which they were handsomely paid.

'Lachie is a local business legend, but dodgy. A man with very twisted morals and his fingers in many pies, I think you say.'

The way Daria uses English idioms sounds almost poetic.

'He is a married man with five children of his own and a nanny to do all the looking after, and a wife who is an eternal mature student. His criminal things mean that he is very wealthy. Obscenely wealthy, I think. More than enough money to pay for sharp lawyers who are bendy.'

I can't help but smile at this slightly bendy use of the vernacular. 'Bent, you mean?'

'Yes, that is what I said.'

Daria continues to explain that the wife is also rumoured to have 'done time' for Lachie, in exchange for a very large diamond ring. Until his arrest he lived just outside of town in a converted Art Deco house, while his brothel workers were kept in poverty.

It is a huge place, like in the movies, with big gates and black windows, a big swimming pool and a line-up of expensive sports cars. 'You get the picture, Louise.'

I certainly do.

Lachie, like Baz and his contemporaries, was a local boy who grew up on the big council estate near the motorway. He started out as a low-level drug dealer who invested his profits in property. He went on to own a substantial portion of the rented housing stock in the city, and then he spread his wings into brothels and night clubs, recruiting innocent young women like Ashley into a seedy underworld of sex crime and drug dependency. He was facing a long time in prison. Ashley's crime of solicitation for prostitution and possession of drugs was a far lesser offence.

It is in the public interest to prosecute the keepers of brothels and those who abuse, harm, exploit, or make a living from the earnings of prostitutes, rather than the prostitutes themselves. Ashley would have been released in a matter of months, but perhaps she knew that being trusted to look after Eden again would be a long and arduous process. Perhaps she also felt that she had let her daughter down so badly that Eden was better off without her.

After rounding up the women in his numerous brothels, police eventually raided Lachie's house and took a hoard of drugs and guns from a hidden strong room in the basement. But his arrest and that discovery of the stronghold were fortuitous – a lucky coincidence for the investigating officer.

'When Lachie asked the policewoman in charge of the raid how she knew where to find those criminal things, she told him that the house was previously owned by friends of her family. She used to play in the basement and remembered it was much bigger than how it looks now. It helped to break the case. That was a strike of luck, I think.'

She means a stroke of luck, but her English is so nearly perfect and this story so unbelievably shocking that now is not the moment for pedantry.

'This Lachie, Baz and a few other gang members all received hefty jail sentences as more evidence came to light. It is a big story, Louise. Lachie was also made responsible for a number of children born to the prostitutes he used in the brothel that were DNA tested to be his. His wife finally left him and she did the hitting of the bottle so all his children were taken into care.'

The Lachie story, as explained by Daria with her various creative touches, feels like a novel. How can this be the reality of anyone's actual life? I began the conversation standing up, but as Daria has been speaking I have gradually sunk back down into my office chair – still out of earshot from Eden, though I can hear the *Peppa Pig* music from time to time. It sounds so incongruous – so childish and innocent compared with what I can only imagine has happened to Eden in all of this. What has she seen and heard? What might she have absorbed, what with all these references to drugs and brothels and prostitution? My goodness. Sometimes I think the world has gone mad. At what point did Lachie, or Baz, or any of these people involved, think that any of this was okay? I wonder what influenced them into becoming these bad people. It really sounds like a Hollywood movie, or maybe a bad version of *The Sopranos*. I suspect we don't know the half of it.

Chapter 11

A pre-meeting is held in my kitchen the next day. Catherine, Daria, and Catherine's manager Chloe, who is a very young woman (younger than either Catherine or Daria), are all in awkward attendance. I wonder if the newly qualified social work graduates become managers just a little too soon. I met one recently who was still living with his parents; not a lot of life experience going on there. It also occurs to me that some of the much younger social workers and managers may still have their own issues going on with 'adults' around them. So, given that the average age of foster carers is 53 years old and rising rapidly, we are more likely to be the same age as their parents – or even older. I wonder if some feel that age difference and are either intimidated by it, or transfer their perceptions of their parents' generation onto foster carers. I would hazard a guess that they do. I also suspect that many of the older, more experienced social workers would not want the role of manager. I can't think of a more stressful position than 'middle manager' – you get pressure from both ends.

We sit round the table while Eden lies on the sofa with her head dangling off the side. I notice a dribble becoming a longer drool of spittle from the corner of her mouth; she looks relaxed. Relaxed enough that I feel able to get up and close the door so she can't hear what we say. Chloe starts the meeting by summarising why we are all here, assigning everyone their roles in an officious way. I want to say that I'm here because I live here, but resist. Sometimes the formality is ridiculous and makes me feel like a naughty schoolgirl, but now is not the time.

Daria asks Catherine what she has managed to do regarding Eden's recent disclosure.

'I have put all the details on Eden's file,' Catherine explains, as though that is job done, case closed.

I watch Daria's face closely as she asks if Catherine has informed the police.

'No, not yet,' Catherine admits. 'I haven't had time. My mother is very ill and I will be leaving tonight to drive to Liverpool to see her.'

Chloe takes over again at that point. 'Yes, that's right. I will inform the relevant authorities on Catherine's behalf, since I will cover the next week while Catherine is on compassionate leave visiting her mother. After all, we only have one mum.'

True. And now Eden's is gone. My blood reaches volcanic boiling point in just one second. I really am about to erupt. Moments like this remind me that some of the personnel working around looked-after children have not got a clue about the fragile nature of what is going on. I am very sorry that Catherine's mother is ill, of course I am, but Eden's mother is dead and another change of personnel isn't helpful for her right now. Changes like this can detract from the vital work that foster carers and adopters do, complicate it and make it more difficult than it needs to be. I don't know what the answer is, I only know that I am incandescent that Eden's loss isn't being acknowledged in the same way. She is still a couple of months away from her sixth birthday. If anyone in this house needs their mother it is her – and that is impossible, of course.

I look across to Daria, who I sense is also simmering beneath her calm surface. We make large angry eyes at each other, then carry on with the meeting as though nothing has happened. I am shaking a fist at the sky in my imagination.

I know I will never forget that comment – *we only have one mum*.

I update Catherine and Chloe on Eden's reaction to the news of her mother's death. We never know what's going on in a child's mind or anyone's. I feel protective of Eden now more than ever, especially with what has gone on in the last few minutes. I hate these meetings. It's always the same old story: we work through a number of possible ideas to help Eden, which all feel like they have come out of a text book devoid of emotional understanding.

'Maybe we need to make decisions about any future work with Eden with her father,' I smile. 'Maybe, in these exceptional circumstances where a child has lost her *one mum*...' I pause to let that comment resonate for a moment; it's unfair to Catherine perhaps, but I can't help myself. 'In these circumstances, maybe he's the answer. I know that he hasn't been involved in Eden's upbringing thus far, but now might be the time he needs to step up.'

'Which brings us to the funeral,' Catherine says. I don't see how it does, quite, but she talks for a moment about the arrangements that have been made so far. 'And we need to talk about who will be taking Eden.'

Chloe says, 'Of course, it's usually the social worker who escorts a child to a funeral, but in this case it would be good if you go as well, Louise, as I haven't met Eden properly yet — she doesn't really know me.'

I look at Daria who, with her big greeny-blue eyes, nods a subtle 'yes'.

So I agree, and ask if Eden's dad will be coming.

'I believe that, yes, he and his parents will be present,' Chloe reports in her unnecessarily formal way that is now really starting to annoy me.

'Good. But, out of interest, why didn't Eden go to Matt when Ashley first went to prison?'

'He didn't know anything about it. He hasn't had any contact with Eden since just after she was born. They'd agreed between them that he wouldn't be part of Eden's life, and he was actually quite difficult to track down.'

'So, how do we manage this? Eden meeting her father – and her paternal grandparents – for the first time, under these highly charged emotional circumstances.'

There is talk of various scenarios, all of which seem to me to be deeply unnatural – and, if I'm honest, some are even faintly ridiculous.

'Can the funeral not be delayed until Eden has actually met her dad and his family – and even Ashley's family, if she has any?' I feel once more as though I am stating the bleeding obvious. Why can no one else see it?

I am relieved when it is agreed that this is, perhaps, an option, and Catherine is tasked with approaching whoever is handling things from Ashley's side to allow this to happen. She looks decidedly uncomfortable with this responsibility.

I pipe up, as I always do, 'It's in the best interests of the child.' I know that I sound like a stuck record at times, but it serves as a reminder that this is the correct mantra from children's social care – and we *all* need to remember that.

Next we clarify the arrangements for meeting Eden's dad. Daria is in charge of the logistics of this, and will liaise with Catherine to see if they can make this happen prior to the funeral. I wonder how he – Matt – must feel about everything that has happened. I know Ashley loved her daughter and I suspect she saw no way out for her or Eden – or maybe she felt that Eden was safe and she herself had nothing to live for. I can't imagine how Ashley felt. I remain convinced that she wasn't a bad woman, just vulnerable as so many are. Especially now that I know about this organised layer of crime that befell them. This Lachie character sounds as though he exploited them all – probably Baz, too. I try to ignore the fact that a few days ago I thought Baz was the bad guy and should live out the rest of his days in prison. But the law doesn't see Baz and Ashley as having been exploited. We are all responsible for our own actions unless there is a good reason why we are not.

While all the formal talk continues I make a silent, snap decision that I will take the children camping this weekend. I am not a natural camper. Okay, if I'm honest I hate being away from my creature comforts. But we will all need a change of scene, especially Eden. I can borrow my friend's camper van and load up the car with the tent and head off to the New Forest. In theory, it will be idyllic.

Lloyd is the natural adventurer in this household: the camper, the sailor, the doer of activities that require 'equipment', the lover of the great outdoors. I have a theory that you need to have grown up with these activities in order to enjoy them as an adult. I didn't; my adopted family did hardly anything at all. I had boyfriends whose whole family sailed for fun. I went along and hung over the side being sick. I went camping with friends and hated it: hours of being cold, wet and muddy – but watching with fascination as everyone around me seemed to love being in this unacceptable state. I like an accessible, clean toilet at the very least It doesn't seem a lot to ask for. But, in the interests of an 'experience', I will put aside all my camping aversions and muck in.

I reveal my nascent idea to Daria after the meeting. An ordeal of sorts that I'm glad is over. Nowadays I have stopped providing biscuits at these events – we don't even get offered a drink when we go to their offices. Call me petty, but hey.

I clear up the kitchen as the social workers pack away their laptops and pens. They all troop towards the garden room to say goodbye to Eden. She is still lying on the sofa, arm hanging off the side, mouth wide open – and now snoring away quite nicely. I give a little laugh and say, 'There you are. That's what she thinks about meetings!'

Actually, it's often what I think of them, too. But, in spite of Catherine's mistimed interruptions and ill-considered decisions, she is only human, she has a sick relative, and Chloe is only doing her job as best she can. Between us we are getting somewhere, and I genuinely feel the love and care from all three women. Ultimately, we do all want the same thing: what's best for Eden. And that makes me happy. It has after all been productive in a number of ways, even if it took us a little while to get there and cut through the formality and bureaucracy to find the common sense.

I see them out, and while Eden is snoozing I take the opportunity to email my editor with some corrections and ideas. I also need to tell Lloyd that we're all going camping this weekend. I'm sure he will be delighted. He's been away so much in recent weeks, and missed out on much of the drama. He will, I am sure, enjoy the family time.

When the children come home from school I run the camping idea past them.

Vincent is the keenest, as his 'Yesssss! Nerf war!' response attests. He clearly sees this as an opportunity to pack his Nerf water guns and torment Lily. Lily in return will threaten near death if he goes anywhere near her. Fun. Jackson is quieter. I look at him, very much now growing into a young man, and ask him directly if he is okay with our proposed adventure.

'Yeah, of course,' he smiles.

But I am not convinced. My tension radar kicks in and I dig a bit deeper.

'Well, I was planning on going to a party, actually, but there will be others. It doesn't matter. And I don't want to miss out on the camping.'

I respond with the usual requests of, where, time, who and which mum do I need to talk to about sleepovers. So far I have not experienced the lies and deceit that the teenage me applied to making sure I went to parties and had sleepovers.

I have a theory (yes, I know, I have a lot of theories) that as parents we don't need to say 'no' all the time – we can find ways to make things work that are mutually acceptable. I just need to know that he is safe.

'It obviously does matter. I think we can make this work and manage both things,' I smile, while noticing his sideburns that I'm absolutely sure were not there last week. 'We'll just camp for a single night.' Which will suit me just fine, but I don't say that.

He looks delighted. 'Amazing! If that's okay with you?'

Eden gets caught up in the general excitement. Vincent explains to her what camping is all about, sensing her confusion. I can see they have a soft spot for each other. Vincent really has been a brilliant big brother these past weeks. I can never predict if the children will get on with our foster children. I have got it totally wrong in the past. I remember one girl who was 14 and got on so well with Vincent back when he was seven. I hadn't expected it at all. She was a tomboy, who would cycle off to the park with him, happy to pack Nerf guns into her backpack and possessing the same ability for crisp-consumption as Vincent. They would have a whale of a time, and then, when they came back, they would sit playing Minecraft together. The age and gender difference was irrelevant. This feels like that same situation, but in reverse. Vincent has revealed a soft, caring side to his nature that I am dazzled by. I am equally entranced by Eden's connection with Vincent – it's lovely to see. Eden is excited about the camping weekend, though 'weekend' is slightly hyperbolic, as it will only be for one night.

Thursday is the appointed day for Eden's first meeting with her father, and it comes round quickly enough. I feel some anticipation, but overall I have a good feeling about this encounter with Matt. I try once again to imagine how he must be feeling. If all is well with Matt and his family, Eden could begin a phased transfer quite quickly – but all the ducks need to be lined up first. It was agreed at the meeting that I wouldn't tell Eden too much before the day, which makes sense. She has enough to think about after all, and her dad could still change his mind and cancel. That would be terrible for her. I don't want to get her hopes up about anything, especially at this fragile time.

In the morning, after the children have all gone to school, I go to wake Eden up. She is already awake, sitting up in bed, bright as a button and reading the book Daria left about rabbits.

I wonder if she really understands what's happened to her mum. After she gets out of bed and follows me to the kitchen for her breakfast, I ask her about the book. She tells me it's about a rabbit that goes into a hole and dies. I ask her about what she understands by the word 'dies'. She looks at me with those knowing eyes and says, 'Mummy,' in a quiet voice that communicates a world of understanding, leaving me in no doubt of her knowledge, and her pain. I feel a big, chunky lump in my throat.

While Eden is busy eating her cereal, I check in with Catherine to see that Matt is still coming to the best of her knowledge.

After breakfast, Eden chooses an outfit. She knows that we are doing something special today, but I haven't told her quite what, yet. Nevertheless, she selects the dress she was saving to see her mum and dresses herself with the same care and attention to detail as she did on that day. Somehow it seems like an act of bravery and I start tearing up at the thought of it.

I get some water and a snack, then we are good to go. We walk to the car. I put her into her car seat. She has the rabbit book open on the same page that she was looking at this morning. I ask her who's in the picture.

She points to one rabbit and speaks, again very quietly. This time she says, 'Daddy'. That's two words already this morning. I don't know if I have packed enough tissues for today's emotional rollercoaster.

We drive up the B road that will take us towards the social services building, with *Girls Aloud* blaring away in the background. Eden is kicking her legs, sometimes into the back of my seat.

'Eden, luvvy,' I sing-song along to fit with the lyrics of the song, 'Can you try and not kick my seat please? It makes me jump.'

She smiles at the idea of me jumping, and so do I. We get to the offices and drive round looking for a parking space. I drive round three times and on the third circuit, sure enough, a car pulls away from a space, leaving it for me to zoom in. Result. I rattle the change in the parking money pot and go and get a ticket. The ticket machine is broken. Right. I look for another; that one is broken too. Hmm. I look at the time: I haven't got enough time left to keep searching for another machine if I want to make this appointment. I decide to write a note to the parking person with an explanation and my phone number and leave caution to the wind. I know I couldn't claim a ticket back from the local authority; blood from stones comes to mind. I help Eden out of the car. As we walk, I check again via text message that her dad is still coming. The answer pings back instantly: 'He's already here'. I hold Eden's hand and guide her over to a wooden bench to sit down for a moment. I look at her gorgeous, trusting face and say, 'We're going to see someone special in a minute.'

She looks at me with those knowing eyes of hers and says, 'DADDY'. It isn't like the occasional words she has said in her quiet half-voice; this is a proper child's voice.

'Yes,' I say, a little taken aback, wondering if she has overheard me talking on the telephone, or if Catherine inadvertently let the cat out of the bag at the meeting earlier in the week. 'How did you know?'

'Mummy told me in my dream.' Her words are matter of fact.

I am floored by that answer, but we have an appointment to keep. I want to ask more. I am very curious about this dream – and amazed by her measured approach, the poise and dignity she demonstrates, the careful selection of that outfit. But there is no time. We walk into the offices, check in at the reception desk and sit down in the waiting area. We are only there a moment before Chloe appears and invites us to follow her.

'Do you know who's here today, Eden?' she asks. I want to tell her to stop using her children's television presenter voice; Eden's too old for it. But of course, she's so young, really. She just has a solemnity beyond her years.

'DADDY,' she responds. Again it is said with an assurance and a volume that is delightful to hear.

I look at Chloe, who smiles back at me. 'Eden's mummy told her that in a dream,' I feel compelled to say.

'Wow, that's wonderful,' says Chloe. 'Let's go and meet him, then!'

We follow Chloe along a corridor into a corporate-style meeting room. It is laid out in a formal arrangement of chairs and tables, and the place where Eden chooses to sit makes it feel as if she is about to chair the whole thing. I wonder that they don't have anything a little more suitable for an occasion like this, perhaps with a sofa or an easy chair, but I guess not.

Thankfully, Eden is too young to understand the room layout and be put off by the position of dominance that she inadvertently occupies by where she sits. I sit down nearby and I feel nervous. I'd quite like some of Eden's calm and poise right now.

Chloe opens a window to release some of the institutional air. I'm grateful. It's hot in here, or my temperature is raised with anxiety. I realise that my concern is on behalf of Eden. I want this to go well for her so much. Chloe leaves us to it while she goes to fetch Matt from wherever he has been waiting. The tension mounts. If I am feeling like this, how must Eden be feeling? I reach across to her and hand her the bag of toys and things to do that I have brought with us in case there is a wait. She pulls out the colouring book and sets out the pencils. I notice that her teddy has been snuck into the bag. Good thinking, Eden. Especially as she was aware of what was happening today. I pull out a tupperware container of grapes and squares of cheese and a bottle of squash. She takes a drink, but doesn't touch the food, even though it is one of her favourite snacks.

Chloe returns and sits down next to Eden. 'Your Daddy is waiting outside to see you. Are you ready to see him?'

Eden looks at me – for reassurance or confirmation, perhaps – and nods.

Chloe leaves the room once more to bring Matt in, which gives me another chance to look at Eden's face. She looks calm – much calmer than me. But at the same time I can tell there is a huge amount going on beneath the surface, as though she is busy in her thoughts.

Through the glass panel in the door I can see people walking about with files and bits of paper. This is the nerve centre of children's social care. It is the place where vital decisions are made and reckonings realised. My own life started off in a file in a cabinet in a building just like this. I existed as a set of paperwork on someone's desk. I hope, with all my heart, that this meeting will be successful and that Eden is removed from the care system so that she can live her life without that stigma hanging round her neck on top of all the trauma she has already experienced.

I bring myself back to the moment, the here and now. I thought Matt was just outside the door, but Chloe is taking her time. Time to look again at Eden. The poker face from that day we first met – only a few months ago, but so much seems to have happened in that time – is gone, replaced by an eager little expression, features open and waiting, despite the hand that has been dealt to her. She has no choice but to trust us – and hopefully Matt, too. I hope to God he's a good man. You never really know, and sometimes when decisions are made for children the financial implications can lead the outcome. It will be much cheaper to place Eden with her dad, out of the over-burdened children's social care system. I try not to think too deeply on this. Sometimes I think I know too much.

I watch as Eden continues to draw, sketching and colouring. I'm the first person to talk of the therapeutic power of art, but I wonder how she can even hold a pencil right now. I watch, but now through eyes that are no longer concentrating on her. I'm focused on the man who is going to walk through that door and perhaps claim his daughter. From the other side of the door I see Chloe lean her hand on the handle. I can vaguely see the outline of a man behind her. She is lingering in the corridor talking to him, their voices muffled through the door and wall so we can hear the cadences but not the words.

Come on!' I say to myself. 'Open the bloody door!' Chloe must have some sense of how unbearable this waiting is.

I notice that Eden too has looked up from her colouring to see the same scene. She must feel this same sense of expectation, surely?

Chloe finally opens the door to reveal Matt.

It is the man in the photograph.

I have no idea how Eden got hold of the picture, or what she knows about her father, but it is definitely him.

Now I watch his face as he sees Eden. I cry. In just a few seconds I have no doubt whatsoever that Matt is going to look after Eden with the love she deserves. He has her curls, though his hair is a much darker nut brown, and his eyes dark brown, too. Eden inherited her mother's eyes. The warmth emanating from his face is unmistakable, though. No one has said a single word, but I am now crying my eyes out. I knew there couldn't be enough tissues for today. I'd go as far as to say I have lost it, actually. I sit with my growing pile of sodden tissues and see that Chloe, too, standing behind Matt, has tears swelling in her eyes. Still no one speaks, but Eden makes a little movement. I dart my gaze towards her and through my blurry vision I watch as she fumbles in the bag and grabs her teddy.

Still nobody speaks. Matt stands there a few paces into the room, and looks as overwhelmed as any of us. With three adults seemingly incapacitated, it is left to Eden to make the first move and break the spell. She slides down from the chair with the teddy bear in her hands and walks slowly towards her father. When she reaches him, she holds out the bear to him. It is washed and fragrant, but worn and well loved, and she places it squarely in his hands. His eyes are full of tears as she hands him the toy. Eden is the only person in the room not weeping.

He strokes the fur and bursts into an anguished sob. 'I got this for you, Eden, when you were a baby.'

She looks up at him. 'I know.'

He doesn't know what to do – to crouch down to her or reach out to pick her up. I feel for him. I feel his hesitation, his lack of knowledge about what is allowed. He looks at Chloe – who is still crying – and asks if he can pick her up.

'Yes, yes. Of course.'

Then he does reach forward, and no coaxing is needed as Eden throws herself into his arms and nestles into his shirt. 'Daddy, Daddy.'

That's it, I'm a complete mess. I move myself to pretend to get something from my bag and to try to give my eyes a rest from crying.

Eden has her father, and her voice.

Chapter 12

We leave Matt and Eden playing and talking with the door open while Chloe and I talk about the plans for getting Eden to live with her dad. My eyes keep flicking to the father and daughter. She's showing him her colouring and chatting away. Chatting! Her voice is gorgeous: rich and resonant. She's not quiet at all – she's funny and lively. I notice a slight lisp in her voice and I hear it in Matt too. I explain to Chloe that I had planned to take all the children to the New Forest this weekend, as a lift for everyone after the sadness of the last few days, but also as a farewell event for Eden.

'The children, especially Vincent, will be sad when she leaves us.'

We have to remember that our children create bonds and connections too. Though not always. My children have demanded that we remove some children from our house in the past, and for a moment I had thought we might get to that when Eden was mistreating Dotty. Of course, the children know it's not that straightforward – but it doesn't stop their feelings and needs.

'Yes, I think that's a good plan,' Chloe agrees. She explains some of the discussions that have taken place this morning before we arrived. Things have moved on fast. From next week, once the funeral is over, we start the phased move of Eden to Matt. He will come next week to our house for tea, then the following week Matt will introduce Eden to her grandparents. Next she will be introduced to his girlfriend who, apparently, is lovely and fully on board with having Eden to live with them.

Chloe seems so much more 'human' today. All that false formality from the other day is gone. She tells me that the grandparents have also stepped up and said that they are happy to help with Eden's care and will offer practical support with school runs and collections while Matt and his girlfriend are working. Chloe goes on to say that from all her investigations, it seems that Ashley had no family of her own left. Her mother died around the time that Ashley started secondary school. She was then brought up by her grandmother who also died – when Ashley was pregnant with Eden.

I hate hearing all this about a woman I never knew who was dealt such a terrible hand. How awful to be pregnant with no partner and no family around you. And Ashley was such a young mum; she was unlikely to have had friends her own age going through anything like what she was going through. How terrible to be all alone, and grieving, when your child comes into the world. What that girl must then have endured doesn't bear thinking about – to end up in the pit of despair that resulted in her taking her own life.

'No wonder she had no way out from the clutches of Lachie and Baz,' I say. 'All alone. No support network. A child to provide for. An easy target for scum like them.'

I love life, but sometimes its unhappinesses distress and overwhelm me. Thank goodness Eden does now have the chance of a family around her.

'Ashley had some good friends from school, apparently, but she lost touch with them after Eden was born. Some of them are devastated by what's happened. It's her best friend who has taken care of all the funeral arrangements, a woman called Kerry who knew very little about Eden's life recently – not since Ashley had taken up with Baz. She blames herself for not doing more in the early stages.'

'Not easy, though, to get involved in all that.'

'No. According to Kerry, she was doing so well bringing up Eden on her own. She was even thinking about going back to college and restarting her education when Eden started school. This Kerry knew Eden and babysat for her so that Ashley could go out – so she also partly blames herself for Ashley even meeting Baz in the first place. She tried hard to intervene in the early stages, but Ashley had seemed so happy when she first got involved with Baz. She really fell for him badly, it seems, and pushed Kerry away once Baz moved in, no longer responding to text messages or wanting to keep in touch. Kerry had no idea things had got so bad until she found out that Ashley had actually gone to prison.'

It's a terrible story of the needless destruction and waste of life.

I continue to watch father and daughter for another lovely moment. I think I already adore Matt: he is fully attentive and already seems devoted to his little girl. The road ahead will not necessarily be straightforward. Eden has plenty of things still to work out. Matt will need to be strong to guide her through the next few years. But how things change over such a short space of time. I am so happy now that I could burst.

Chloe is called away by another social worker, presumably to another crisis or another tragedy. I sit on an old brown stacker chair just outside the meeting room and call Daria who, true to form, answers immediately – as if she has been waiting for the phone to ring. With joy in my voice I tell her all about Matt. I give her a blow-by-blow account of this magical meeting, including my own hopeless-to-control emotional reaction to what I witnessed. I feel so privileged sometimes to be part of the good moments – and, to be honest, it makes up for all the hard times and difficulties I have looking after other people's offspring in a system that is broken and sometimes feels cold and heartless. Today I have seen nothing but love and care from the staff, and from Eden's newly found dad.

'Oh, I think I deserve a big glass of wine when I get home.'

'Yes, you do, Louise,' Daria agrees, making me realise that I have actually voiced that private thought out loud.

Chapter 13

It's Friday morning and I feel shattered. Totally wiped out. All that emotion from yesterday has left me feeling utterly drained. Never mind, there is an adventure to be had.

I set about preparing the camping gear. I have to say, this is really not my thing. Did I mention that? I asked Lloyd to prepare a list. He dutifully obliged, but it is long and yet seems not to contain half of what my brain says we will need. So now I have been rummaging around in the shed for tents, torches, balls and bats for what feels like hours. In the bottom of the airing cupboard are all the clean rolled sleeping bags. Out they come. I know that for just one night and two days this is going to be a monumental amount of effort. I make a mental note to get the children to bring their pillows in the car. I pack sleeping clothes, though I know that it will be only Lily who will really care and bother to change into them. The boys will go stinky. When I think I have everything ready, I pile both the necessary and the unnecessary by the back door in the garden room.

Why did I think this would be a good idea again? I will pop out later to get food. There is going to have to be camp cooking of some description. It would cost a small fortune to take this many children to the pub for dinner, so instead I think of things we can cook on the gas fire. The children asked for marshmallows. I hate to be the party pooper, and I'm usually not, but I have been cautious about these ever since I did my first-aid course last year. Too many children die from choking on fluffy marshmallows that expand and get stuck in their throats, apparently. I plan to take some Rich Tea biscuits along to sandwich the marshmallows in. That reminds me to check the first-aid kit. For one night, this really seems like a substantial amount of effort. It had better all be worth it.

Eden is in the garden room having a tea party with her teddy and the dogs.

'You okay, Eden?' I call out to her, just checking in.

I hear her lovely little voice, with its delightful, slight lisp, call back. 'Ye-es,' she says, very simply, but as though it is the most natural thing in the world to return my question.

I am so happy just to keep listening to her voice, and marvel at her composure.

I make a few calls to Chloe and Daria. Daria is as overjoyed as I am. She has checked the unlocked file on Eden which is now nearly complete. Chloe has taken over from Catherine fully and has been very thorough and compassionate in her work. She has compiled a good comprehensive file with lots of lovely handwritten comments from the social workers who spent time with Eden.

I too will write a letter to Eden for her to read in future life. It's part of 'My Story', the box of memories that we have collected from her stay; all the little comments I have made along the way are gathered together in a notebook. What comes through most strongly as we flick back through it is all her drawing, but also remarks about her kindness and the little thoughtful things that she has done along the way. The children have written cards, and Lily has inked a long letter about being in care, sharing her own experiences, and congratulating Eden on how wonderful it is to find her daddy. Lily, though undoubtedly happy here – and I could never imagine her living anywhere else – likes to think about being in the care system, and reflect on the realities of what that means. I think it's partly because she has watched the film versions of *Matilda* and *Annie* so many times that she can recite the script. She is clearly drawn to those characters because of their orphan status but also their fairytale endings. At the moment she is still waiting for her billionaire Daddy Warbucks to appear on the scene – and I'm certainly no Miss Honey. I will need to do some work on this later on, I suspect. Or maybe not – she may just move it on herself as she gets older and realises that films are films and the actors are pretending.

It is early Saturday morning and the car and camper-van are finally packed and ready to go. Lloyd is driving the campervan. I would far rather be in the car with my music – and a gearbox I know well. Interestingly, the boys ask to come with me and the girls with Lloyd. The girls are still on catch-up with what life can offer. They jump at every new excitement, whereas the boys, perhaps because they are my birth children and have had many experiences and been safe and secure all their lives, are quite cool about things. They will sit with their headphones on, listening to music or gaming. What vehicle they are travelling in is an irrelevance. Jackson is a little tired this morning, but he survived his party and is playing the role of dutiful son in gratitude for having been allowed to go.

The dogs are also having a little minibreak, visiting Kate, my wonderful neighbour who looks after the pets and house if we go away. We all need someone like this in our lives to help keep things moving along smoothly.

We set off on our journey to the New Forest. It's a long drive and I am more than a little frustrated at how slow I'm having to go to stay with the camper van. We stop at a big service station on the way. It has a large grass area; maybe the children can run off a bit of energy that has been charging up while they have been stuck in the car.

Not a chance.

Instead they go to the loo then ask for a KFC. Of course they do. With buckets of chicken covered in salt, and diet coke in outsize cups, we head to the park bench and I watch them devour the lot in nanoseconds. There is a lovely atmosphere amongst them; Vincent keeps asking Eden questions just to hear her voice. He is as fascinated by it as I am. She evidently adores him and is happy to oblige after her months of silence. Chloe and I have agreed that as part of the phased transfer over to Matt, it is important that we involve the children – especially Vincent, who will be hardest hit by Eden's departure.

As we crawl along in traffic outside the New Forest, I look in the rearview mirror and see two very happy girls sitting up high in the campervan, on top of the world. I suspect Lloyd is being subjected to more Girls Aloud, perhaps alternating with some of Lily's emo music – maybe Slipknot. Lloyd will love that. Not. I smile to myself as I tune in to Radio 4's *Saturday Live*, an altogether more pleasing prospect that I settle back to enjoy. The boys don't care – they are plugged back in to their own thing. I hear the dulcet tones of the Reverend Richard Coles – who used to be in The Communards, a band I remember dancing to in the early eighties with my friend Lisa. That sets me off on another trip down memory lane. I remember that while we were getting ready to go out, she would steal her mum's vodka and we would make short work of it, grimacing as we knocked it back. We were usually a mess before we got to the party – the getting ready was as much fun as the party itself. I am so conflicted, sometimes, about this sort of thing. I hope that Jackson enjoyed himself at his party last night, but I don't like to think of him doing the same things that I did. It's a dichotomy I can't explain. But I love thinking about the happier parts of my childhood: it was usually time spent with my friends, not my adopted family.

Finally we drive down a little road, passing along the unfenced moorland and heathland where we catch our first sight of the famous New Forest ponies. The boys begin to pay attention to the scene before them, drinking in the differences in the scenery that contrast with home. I think it's always exciting driving towards a new destination. I still feel it when we drive to the beach and you get that first glimpse of the sea in the distance and your heart is full of excitement and joy. Vincent thinks he spots a deer behind some ferns; Jackson is convinced it is just another pony.

It takes us a few minutes to locate the campsite itself. I lead the way to our spot on the camping field, a relatively secluded nook in one corner, backed by a woody hedgerow, not too far from a grand oak tree that has a tyre swing attached to it. I instantly check to see how close we are to the loos and showers, and am satisfied. I will never be able to entirely rough it – it's just not my thing – but Lloyd and the children would be quite happy to.

Under the close supervision of Lloyd, we begin to set up the tents. Eden has given herself the job of chief den-maker. She takes over most of the tent that she is sharing with Lily and places her colouring books and toys out on display, carefully arranging them around her sleeping bag and blanket that she has spread out across one corner. Lily moans about the lack of remaining space and decides that she will take over the porch area to get her fair share, but can't stay moody for long because they are so excited to have their own house – albeit one made of canvas rather than bricks and mortar.

Finally, our little hamlet of tents is complete to everyone's satisfaction.

Oh, how I love camping! For a moment or two, at least.

Next we decide to go for a walk. I lock up any valuables into the boot of the car as we head out to the woods to see the ponies close up. The air is lovely and the sun is strong and vibrant. I fuss over Eden's skin, insisting that she wears factor 50 sunscreen. She is not impressed. Since meeting her daddy she has transformed into a bundle of confidence and joy – and self-assertion. To be honest, she hasn't stopped chatting. We have running monologues on the shape of trees, or clouds in the sky. 'Look at this, Louise,' she will call when she spots an interesting flower or creature. I am not a particular fan of minibugs of any description, but I have to pretend that I am fascinated by earwigs and woodlice and even ants. When she asks for something out loud, we all jump to it, rushing to be the one to hand her the ketchup or pass the milk from the fridge. It's a natural reaction to the weeks and weeks of silence, I think.

As she protests at the application of the cream, Vincent jokingly says, 'Wow, Eden. It was so much quieter before. Can't we have the old Eden back?'

She gets the joke, makes a face to tell him exactly what she thinks of his humour, and carries on talking about ponies and how much she wants one of her own. 'I might take one home with me.'

It's truly wonderful to see. I love that she will now give as good as she gets.

Our walk takes us into the village to find ice creams and maybe a pub or cafe for drinks. They will have to wait for their dinner, and I have a boot load of snacks. I will keep them locked up in the car or the locusts will demolish them. By locusts, I don't mean that the New Forest has some terrible infestation – that's mainly the boys with their hollow legs. I am convinced Vincent has grown a foot in the last month.

Back at the site I watch Eden skip around the field. We find a play park in the next field beyond the tyre swing. It's dusty with dry ground from all the good weather. She climbs up the ladder of the slide and slides down. I can hear the backs of her legs squeak on the metal. Ouch, I think, but she laughs and laughs. I think of the joy she will bring to Matt's life in the coming years now that he will have the opportunity to watch her grow up and flourish. I believe that he will treasure her. How could he not?

Vincent holds her hand and takes her to the swings. He calls out to me to push him – something he hasn't done for years. I push him as high as I am prepared to go, his long limbs flailing with the momentum. I watch Eden, who I now insist wears a hat to protect her from the sun, much to her disgust. She spins round and round, clanking the chains of her swing. She watches Vincent coil the chain and then let go, whizzing round like a salad spinner. She thinks this is hilarious and wants to have a go herself, squealing in delight as she is let go. Eventually we head back to our tents and set about making dinner. I am totally enjoying the relaxed atmosphere and put all my worries about work deadlines and paintings to one side to enjoy the moment. Who knows, perhaps I could get into this camping lark after all? I have a bag of Kettle chips and sour cream and chive dips that I put out while I cook. They love them, and perform the locust routine. One bag is clearly not enough.

'Tough,' I say, but bring out the breadsticks so that they can finish up the dips.

We heat up the pre-made chili con carne (I have been very organised to make this trip as easy as possible) and eat it with a lovely buttered French baguette, fresh from the village store. Once the meal is over and I have cleared all the plates and pans away, I bring out the cakes, biscuits and sweets.

We sit around telling stories and making dares. The boys want to play hide and seek in the dusky dark. Eden thinks this is a wonderful idea and partners up with Vincent, of course. The rest of us are designated seekers and sit on the blankets to dutifully count to 40 with our eyes closed. Our counting is loud and rhythmic, and we hear giggles as they move away from us. When we reach the magic number, we start looking for Eden and Vincent.

We look and look and look.

We search here and there and everywhere until I genuinely get worried that something has really happened to them. Have there been abductions in the New Forest before? How deep is that lake? I can feel my stress levels increase.

I look at the panic emerging in Lloyd's face. It mirrors my own and only serves to intensify my mounting anxiety. We move fast around the campsite, calling out their names, panicky and fear-edged now. This goes on for ages; Jackson and Lily partner up and begin to search the other side of the campsite more systematically.

I am beginning to feel that fear: the fear that every parent knows. The fear I once felt when I lost the boys in Portsmouth Historical Dockyard when I took them to see the Mary Rose. I lost them both for only a few minutes and I was a mess.

Eventually I hear, 'Mum.'

It's Vincent's voice, thank God. I turn round to see him sitting on the ground behind a tree. I walk towards him and he is smiling, blissfully unaware of all the panic he has just caused.

Eden is fast asleep on the ground next to him with her head resting against his leg.

'I didn't want to wake her, Mum. She looks so peaceful.'

He must see my anxious face in spite of the darkness. 'I texted Dad to let him know where we were so you wouldn't worry.'

Lloyd, just behind me, checks his phone and rolls his eyes. 'Sorry, Vince.'

I drink in the gorgeous sight in front of us. It is like a scene from *Babes in the Woods*. I take a photo on my phone; I think this will be a lovely picture to put in Eden's memory box. A moment suspended in time. No claustrophobic wardrobe, here.

In a few days' time she will be attending the funeral of her mother.

But for now, she can sleep safe and free beneath the stars.

Epilogue

The phased return is a success. We all get along well, and Eden has been back for a couple of sleepovers, which might not have been able to happen if things had been different. If she had still been fostered, she would not be able to stay in a room with Lily – because Lily, though now adopted, was fostered with us, too. We have a new placement, just a temporary one – a teenage girl who is a bit of a pickle – but having Eden to stay gives the other children a positive occupation while I spend my time with the new girl.

I have spent many hours on the phone to Matt, who is now a new father of twin boys. He is doing everything he can for Eden – who has had her own ups and downs, as was only to be expected. As she has got older, the realisation that her mum is dead and killed herself in prison is a hard one to carry. I strongly believe that we need to tell our children the truth – not in a way that deliberately hurts them, but in a way that allows them to know and understand the fractured reality of their lives.

Matt told me about Ashley, and all about how things were between them. He had been madly in love with her when they first met, but had no intention of having a baby. He was due to go travelling with his friends. They had all been saving up; he had been working in a bar in his village when he met Ashley. He said that she was fun and kind, but they had already drifted apart before he went to Australia – going their separate ways as the relationship took its natural course, though they remained friends.

She told him while he was away that she was pregnant. He was initially surprised to hear it because they had always been very careful. His mum was the office manager in the town's family planning unit, so he definitely knew how to be careful, and he thought he had been. His friends and family encouraged him to stay on his travels, especially since there was no hope of rekindling the relationship. His parents took care of the financial arrangements to ensure that Eden was provided for, and though they wanted to meet their grandchild they understood that it might complicate things further for them to be in her life.

While Matt was away he put Ashley and the baby to one side, continuing to live his life as though nothing had ever happened. When he came back he went to see Ashley, just once. She had given birth to little Eden by then. He was sad, but they had made the decision to move on, and he knew he could not be a dad at only 18 years old. He would have been hopeless in the role. He had plans of his own, and was no longer in love with Ashley the way he had once been. She seemed to be managing well and enjoying motherhood and, perhaps selfishly as he now sees, he left her to it. That was the last he knew until he was contacted by the authorities as next of kin on Ashley's death. He feels guilty for not being in touch all that time, and wishes that he had been there to take care of Eden when Ashley went to prison.

He is now a fully qualified tree surgeon and, while he learned the trade through working for someone else, he is now setting up on his own. He has a lovely girlfriend, mother of his twins, who I also now know and feel very fond of. They are a lovely little family. Matt's family have also been great – his mum in particular, who retired around the time of Ashley's death. She had been planning to take up golf, but changed her plans abruptly and has instead made herself emotionally and physically available for Eden and Matt.

Eden is so fortunate that she has a loving family around her now. I know that her mum loved her and was a good person who made some wrong choices and was manipulated under terrible circumstances.

Before Ashley died she wrote a beautiful letter to Eden, and a note to Matt. The autopsy report for Ashley showed that she had been on an emotional decline since her arrest and charge for soliciting for prostitution. She had reported that she was having suicidal thoughts to the prison doctor – who did not act upon it quickly enough. He had offered her medication for postnatal depression. This was evidently a misdiagnosis; Eden was five years old by the time Ashley went to prison, and it was clear to all who knew her that she was depressed because of what had happened to her, the way the course of her life had changed so dramatically, and the gradual build-up of abuse that she had experienced. She was also dangerously, almost debilitatingly reliant on psychic readings and tarot cards. She felt that her destiny was bleak. She missed her daughter and knew that she had let Eden down. I was shown the letter. I needed those damn tissues again. It said this:

Eden,

When you read this you will be grown up and having a life of your own. I hope that your daddy, Matt, has been looking after you. Your daddy is a good man and loves you very much. I loved your daddy at first, too, but it didn't work out as I had hoped. No one's fault. We were both very young. He came to visit you when you were born and gave you Ted – your favourite teddy. I wonder if you still have him?

When I was pregnant with you I was so excited. I had a very good pregnancy and you were a good baby. A very good baby – everyone who ever met you said so. I gave birth to you in St Angela's hospital. I have kept all your precious bits and pieces from your birth and a baby book with all your milestones. You were born at 8.08 am – an easy delivery according to the nurse, but for me it was a shock. I had no idea what it would be like because I had no one to tell me. It didn't matter, because when you were brought to me I took one look at you and fell in love. You were the most beautiful thing I had ever seen.

I took you home but I was all on my own. We had lost my grandma earlier in the year. I am so sad that you never got to meet her. I loved her so deeply. She was very much my rock after my mummy died a few years before. By the time you came along your daddy had gone away and I was still grieving for Nana. I was lonely, and I didn't know what I was doing, and it was hard to know how to look after you. You made it easy, though, and I loved every single moment that we had together before I messed up. You were the apple of my eye, the reason I got up every morning.

I stayed lonely and needed some grown-up company. I was just 19 years old on your first birthday and my friends were all having lives of their own, careers, relationships. Maybe for a while I think I became depressed, but I was always happy to be with you, my little angel. In trying to find that adult company I lost my way and got involved with people who were bad. I didn't know that they were bad at first. I got things wrong. Baz and I were star-crossed lovers who should never have met. I did some things that I am not proud of. And I put you in danger because of it. I can never forgive myself for that.

You, my angel, went into foster care. Your social worker showed me photos of you playing with two little brown dogs. I liked seeing that picture, you looked so happy. What happened to me is my own fault. I believed in magic and I wanted magical things to happen. The reality is that we have to reap what we sow, and I made some terrible mistakes that have cost me dearly. I don't want them to cost you any more than they already have. I lost you and, although I am not here now, I want you to know that I love you, Eden, so much. You are, without doubt, the best thing that happened to me. You are the good thing that I have left behind.

I love you to the moon and back, and back again.

Be a good girl and work hard at school, and please don't make the same mistakes as me.

Love

Mum XXXXX

One day, when she is ready, Matt will show her the letter.

Much groundwork needs to be done first. Ashley, like so many young women, became vulnerable. She needed her mum and grandmother. She lost her boyfriend and gained a baby. Ashley was a good young woman who needed to be loved. Baz, who is still in prison, exploited her for his own gain, but neither of them were as bad as Lachie, who looked after his own children, sent them to the most expensive schools he could and gave them everything money could buy – but knowingly let Eden live without her mum because of the danger he put Ashley in.

Matt has had many dark days trying to absorb the situation, feeling guilt for Ashley and his part in her story, along with a father's worry and love for Eden. After getting to know them, I would say Eden has a better chance than many of having a good life with a sparkling future ahead of her. Life is never straightforward. We are all prone to being 'human', but her humans now are caring and kind.

Eden is doing well at school; she is described as sensitive and funny. Apparently she has a sixth sense: she can see spirits and ghosts. Matt is keeping this under control and wonders how much was passed onto her by her mum, who apparently could not make even a simple decision without the paid advice of a clairvoyant. She never knew that 'Christine' was a computer, generating readings based on algorithms that had nothing to do with the stars and everything to do with profiteering from vulnerable individuals.

Eden's world is never going to be a paradise, though. I don't know if Eden will ever get over her fear of wardrobes and enclosed spaces. I suspect not. The psychologist is working with her to help her to understand what happened, why she has the fears, and how she can deal with them in day-to-day life.

Perhaps we will never know, entirely, what happened while she was inside her wooden prison. What she has revealed so far is that the first time she called out to her mum, Lachie poured beer through the cracks at the top of the wardrobe. As time went on he started pouring in boiling water to shut her up. No one heard her screams. She has explained that she could see quite clearly out from the wardrobe doors where they met in the middle, but has not yet spoken about what she saw. Baz and Lachie and other men did 'bad things', in her words, to her mum. Undoubtedly she witnessed many things that she shouldn't have, given the toxic environment she was living in at the end. There have been no repeats of Eden trying to 'inflict' the same kind of behaviour on anyone else, which may have been what was happening with the dogs and pouring water over Hueydewey – a complex echo of mistreating the things that she loves and identifies with, in the same way she perhaps felt was done to her.

Lachie was up for so many criminal counts in the final reckoning that repeatedly pouring boiling water onto a defenceless, imprisoned child didn't come close to making the charge sheets.

Though perhaps that was the biggest crime of all.

Acknowledgements

I owe the greatest thanks to a man I never knew.

At 9 years of age I went on a school trip to the Tate Gallery. A small crowd had gathered round the Carl Andre, Equivalent VIII (aka Bricks) sculpture. I stood invisibly, or that's what I thought and listened to the adults talk about the work "Is it art?" they were saying. I had never heard such a conversation, I was fascinated. An American man who I thought was a beautiful hippy-looking dude spoke so knowingly about art. I was fascinated and terrified. I was in this incredible building feeling as I usually did, that I was not entitled to anything. The American man looked directly at me and said "Art is for everyone". There are some adults who are able to 'see' children, to intuitively understand and recognise their souls, these adults give generously and want nothing in return. That glorious man changed my life, because after he said that it dawned on me that I was an everyone.

I became an artist.

Thank you to my beautiful blended family, Lloyd, Jackson, Vincent, Taryn, Chloe and Margaret. To Millie and Mitchel and welcome baby Maeve, Poppy, Lola, Ava and Blossom.

Kate my great dog walking friend, who explains the countryside to me. Ronnie for your wisdom. Jo Sollis my wonderful editor who encourages my voice. Mel for all your magic and Mirror Books for supporting my work. Jane Graham-Maw my very special agent. Theresa whose creativity and knowledge is second to none – and our loyal reading trio: Catherine for her forthright consideration of emotional impact; Alexandra for her wise structural and narrative advice; and Karen for her sharp-eyed, sensitive close-reading. You are all invaluable to the process.

Also by Mirror Books

Stella's Story
Louise Allen

*"Stella is just like a tiny bird. This is my first impression of her.
A quiet little sparrow of a girl."*

In the first of a new series *'Thrown Away Children'*, foster mother Louise Allen tells the true story of Stella, a young girl scarred by an abusive past.

Named for the lager that christened her, Stella's life is characterised by dysfunction and neglect. Her mother abandons her as a newborn and in the 'care' of her father, Stella is left with no food, water, clothes or warmth.

Louise becomes Stella's foster carer and is determined to give the girl a better life. But when Stella has a startling response to having her photo taken, it is clear that the effects of her abuse run deep.

MIRROR BOOKS

Also by Mirror Books

Abby's Story
Louise Allen

She doesn't want this baby.
She can't look after this baby.
She will never be able to love this baby.

Little Abby's life begins badly, then just gets worse.

Now foster carer Louise and her family must help her to deal
with the truth about her past, to give her the chance of a future.

The second book in the series
THROWN AWAY CHILDREN

mm
B

MIRROR BOOKS